Marx
Abbott
Hardy
Defoe
Melville
Montaigne
Machiavelli
Haggard
Chesterton
Cooper
Emerson
Joyce
Austen
Hugo
Eliot
Grimm
Carroll
Christie
Stoker
Molière
Wilde
Maupassant
Byron
Schiller
Engels
Garnett
Einstein
Fitzgerald
Hawthorne
Smith
Kafka
Goethe
Dostoyevsky
Cotton
Hall
Baum
Kipling
Doyle
Willis
Leslie
Dumas
Henry
Nietzsche
Flaubert
Turgenev
Balzac
Stockton
Vatsyayana
Crane
Burroughs
Whitman
Verne
Curtis
Tocqueville
Gogol
Vinci
Homer
Widger
Tolstoy
Busch
Darwin
Thoreau
Potter
Freud
Zola
Twain
Plato
Scott
Lawrence
Kant
Jowett
Stevenson
Dickens
Andersen
Cervantes
Burton
Hesse
Harte
London
Descartes
Poe
Aristotle
Wells
Voltaire
Hale
James
Hastings
Cooke
Bunner
Shakespeare
Richter
Chambers
Irving
da
Chekhov
Benedict
Doré
Swift
Dante
Shaw
Wodehouse
Alcott
Pushkin
Newton

tredition®

tredition was established in 2006 by Sandra Latusseck and Soenke Schulz. Based in Hamburg, Germany, tredition offers publishing solutions to authors and publishing houses, combined with worldwide distribution of printed and digital book content. tredition is uniquely positioned to enable authors and publishing houses to create books on their own terms and without conventional manufacturing risks.

For more information please visit: www.tredition.com

TREDITION CLASSICS

This book is part of the TREDITION CLASSICS series. The creators of this series are united by passion for literature and driven by the intention of making all public domain books available in printed format again - worldwide. Most TREDITION CLASSICS titles have been out of print and off the bookstore shelves for decades. At tredition we believe that a great book never goes out of style and that its value is eternal. Several mostly non-profit literature projects provide content to tredition. To support their good work, tredition donates a portion of the proceeds from each sold copy. As a reader of a TREDITION CLASSICS book, you support our mission to save many of the amazing works of world literature from oblivion. See all available books at www.tredition.com.

Project Gutenberg

The content for this book has been graciously provided by Project Gutenberg. Project Gutenberg is a non-profit organization founded by Michael Hart in 1971 at the University of Illinois. The mission of Project Gutenberg is simple: To encourage the creation and distribution of eBooks. Project Gutenberg is the first and largest collection of public domain eBooks.

Reminiscences of Tolstoy

Graf Ilia Lvovich Tolstoi

Imprint

This book is part of TREDITION CLASSICS

Author: Graf Ilia Lvovich Tolstoi
Cover design: Buchgut, Berlin – Germany

Publisher: tredition GmbH, Hamburg - Germany
ISBN: 978-3-8424-3873-6

www.tredition.com
www.tredition.de

REMINISCENCES OF TOLSTOY

BY HIS SON,

Count Ilya Tolstoy

Translated By George Calderon

Contents

REMINISCENCES OF TOLSTOY (Part I.)

IN one of his letters to his great-aunt, Alexandra Andreyevna Tolstoy, my father gives the following description of his children:

The eldest [Sergei] is fair-haired and good-looking; there is something weak and patient in his expression, and very gentle. His laugh is not infectious; but when he cries, I can hardly refrain from crying, too. Every one says he is like my eldest brother.

I am afraid to believe it. It is too good to be true. My brother's chief characteristic was neither egotism nor self-renunciation, but a strict mean between the two. He never sacrificed himself for any one else; but not only always avoided injuring others, but also interfering with them. He kept his happiness and his sufferings entirely to himself.

Ilya, the third, has never been ill in his life; broad-boned, white and pink, radiant, bad at lessons. Is always thinking about what he is told not to think about. Invents his own games. Hot-tempered and violent, wants to fight at once; but is also tender-hearted and very sensitive. Sensuous; fond of eating and lying still doing nothing.

Tanya [Tatyana] is eight years old. Every one says that she is like Sonya, and I believe them, although I am pleased about that, too; I believe it only because it is obvious. If she had been Adam's eldest daughter and he had had no other children afterward, she would have passed a wretched childhood. The greatest pleasure that she has is to look after children.

The fourth is Lyoff. Handsome, dexterous, good memory, graceful. Any clothes fit him as if they had been made for him. Everything that others do, he does very skilfully and well. Does not understand much yet.

The fifth, Masha [Mary] is two years old, the one whose birth nearly cost Sonya her life. A weak and sickly child. Body white as milk, curly white hair; big, queer blue eyes, queer by reason of their deep, serious expression. Very intelligent and ugly. She will be one of the riddles; she will suffer, she will seek and find nothing, will always be seeking what is least attainable.

The sixth, Peter, is a giant, a huge, delightful baby in a mob-cap, turns out his elbows, strives eagerly after something. My wife falls into an ecstasy of agitation and emotion when she holds him in her arms; but I am completely at a loss to understand. I know that he has a great store of physical energy, but whether there is any purpose for which the store is wanted I do not know. That is why I do not care for children under two or three; I don't understand.

This letter was written in 1872, when I was six years old. My recollections date from about that time. I can remember a few things before.

FAMILY LIFE IN THE COUNTRY

FROM my earliest childhood until the family moved into Moscow—that was in 1881—all my life was spent, almost without a break, at Yasnaya Polyana.

This is how we live. The chief personage in the house is my mother. She settles everything. She interviews Nikolai, the cook, and orders dinner; she sends us out for walks, makes our shirts, is always nursing some baby at the breast; all day long she is bustling about the house with hurried steps. One can be naughty with her, though she is sometimes angry and punishes us.

She knows more about everything than anybody else. She knows that one must wash every day, that one must eat soup at dinner, that one must talk French, learn not to crawl about on all fours, not to put one's elbows on the table; and if she says that one is not to go out walking because it is just going to rain, she is sure to be right, and one must do as she says.

Papa is the cleverest man in the world. He always knows everything. There is no being naughty with HIM. When he is up in his study "working," one is not allowed to make a noise, and nobody may go into his room. What he does when he is at "work," none of us know. Later on, when I had learned to read, I was told that papa was a "writer."

This was how I learned. I was very pleased with some lines of poetry one day, and asked my mother who wrote them. She told me they were written by Pushkin, and Pushkin was a great writer. I was vexed at my father not being one, too. Then my mother said that my father was also a well-known writer, and I was very glad indeed.

At the dinner-table papa sits opposite mama and has his own round silver spoon. When old Natalia Petrovna, who lives on the floor below with great-aunt Tatyana Alexandrovna, pours herself out a glass of kvass, he picks it up and drinks it right off, then says, "Oh, I'm so sorry, Natalia Petrovna; I made a mistake!" We all laugh delightedly, and it seems odd that papa is not in the least afraid of Natalia Petrovna. When there is jelly for pudding, papa says it is good for gluing paper boxes; we run off to get some paper, and papa makes it into boxes. Mama is angry, but he is not afraid of her either. We have the gayest times imaginable with him now and then. He can ride a horse better and run faster than anybody else, and there is no one in the world so strong as he is.

He hardly ever punishes us, but when he looks me in the eyes he knows everything that I think, and I am frightened. You can tell stories to mama, but not to papa, because he will see through you at once. So nobody ever tries.

Besides papa and mama, there was also Aunt Tatyana Alexandrovna Yergolsky. In her room she had a big eikon with a silver mount. We were very much afraid of this eikon, because it was very old and black.

When I was six, I remember my father teaching the village children. They had their lessons in "the other house," 1 where Alexey Stepanytch, the bailiff, lived, and sometimes on the ground floor of the house we lived in.

There were a great number of village children who used to come. When they came, the front hall smelled of sheepskin jackets; they were taught by papa and Seryozha and Tanya and Uncle Kostya all at once. Lesson-time was very gay and lively.

The children did exactly as they pleased, sat where they liked, ran about from place to place, and answered questions not one by one, but all together, interrupting one another, and helping one another to recall what they had read. If one left out a bit, up jumped another and then another, and the story or sum was reconstructed by the united efforts of the whole class.

What pleased my father most about his pupils was the picturesqueness and originality of their language. He never wanted a literal repetition of bookish expressions, and particularly encouraged every one to speak "out of his own head." I remember how once he stopped a boy who was running into the next room.

"Where are YOU off to?" he asked.

"To uncle, to bite off a piece of chalk." 2

"Cut along, cut along! It's not for us to teach them, but for them to teach."

THE SERVANTS IN THE HOUSE

WHEN my father married and brought home his young and inexperienced bride, Sofya Andreyevna, to Yasnaya Polyana, Nikolai Mikhailovitch Rumyantsef was already established as cook. Before my father's marriage he had a salary of five rubles a month; but when my mother arrived, she raised him to six, at which rate he continued the rest of his days; that is, till somewhere about the end of the eighties. He was succeeded in the kitchen by his son, Semyon Nikolayevitch, my mother's godson, and this worthy and beloved man, companion of my childish games, still lives with us to this day. Under my mother's supervision he prepared my father's vegetarian diet with affectionate zeal, and without him my father would very likely never have lived to the ripe old age he did.

Agafya Mikhailovna was an old woman who lived at first in the kitchen of "the other house" and afterward on the home farm. Tall and thin, with big, thoroughbred eyes, and long, straight hair, like a witch, turning gray, she was rather terrifying, but more than anything else she was queer.

Once upon a time long ago she had been housemaid to my great-grandmother, Countess Pelageya Nikolayevna Tolstoy, my father's grandmother, nee Princess Gortchakova. She was fond of telling about her young days. She would say:

I was very handsome. When there were gentlefolks visiting at the big house, the countess would call me, 'Gachette [Agafya], femme de chambre, apportez-moi un mouchoir!' Then I would say, 'Toute suite, Madame la Comtesse!' And every one would be staring at me, and couldn't take their eyes off. When I crossed over to the annex, there they were watching to catch me on the way. Many a time have I tricked them—ran round the other way and jumped over the ditch. I never liked that sort of thing any time. A maid I was, a maid I am.

After my grandmother's death, Agafya Mikhailovna was sent on to the home farm for some reason or other, and minded the sheep. She got so fond of sheep that all her days after she never would touch mutton.

After the sheep, she had an affection for dogs, and that is the only period of her life that I remember her in.

There was nothing in the world she cared about but dogs. She lived with them in horrible dirt and smells, and gave up her whole mind and soul to them. We always had setters, harriers, and borzois, and the whole kennel, often very numerous, was under Agafya Mikhailovna's management, with some boy or other to help her, usually one as clumsy and stupid as could be found.

There are many interesting recollections bound up with the memory of this intelligent and original woman. Most of them are associated in my mind with my father's stories about her. He could always catch and unravel any interesting psychological trait, and these traits, which he would mention incidentally, stuck firmly in my mind. He used to tell, for instance, how Agafya Mikhailovna complained to him of sleeplessness.

"Ever since I can remember her, she has suffered from 'a birch-tree growing inside me from my belly up; it presses against my chest, and prevents my breathing.'

"She complains of her sleeplessness and the birch-tree and says: 'There I lay all alone and all quiet, only the clock ticking on the wall: "Who are you? What are you? Who are you? What are you?" And I began to think: "Who am I? What am I?" and so I spent the whole night thinking about it.'

"Why, imagine this is Socrates! 'Know thyself,'" said my father, telling the story with great enthusiasm.

In the summer-time my mother's brother, Styopa (Stephen Behrs), who was studying at the time in the school of jurisprudence, used to come and stay with us. In the autumn he used to go wolf-hunting with my father and us, with the borzois, and Agafya Mikhailovna loved him for that.

Styopa's examination was in the spring. Agafya Mikhailovna knew about it and anxiously waited for the news of whether he had got through.

Once she put up a candle before the eikon and prayed that Styopa might pass. But at that moment she remembered that her borzois had got out and had not come back to the kennels again.

"Saints in heaven! they'll get into some place and worry the cattle and do a mischief!" she cried. "'Lord, let my candle burn for the dogs to come back quick, and I'll buy another for Stepan Andreyevitch.' No sooner had I said this to myself than I heard the dogs in the porch rattling their collars. Thank God! they were back. That's what prayer can do."

Another favorite of Agafya Mikhailovna was a young man, Misha Stakhovitch, who often stayed with us.

"See what you have been and done to me, little Countess!" she said reproachfully to my sister Tanya: "you've introduced me to Mikhail Alexandrovitch, and I've fallen in love with him in my old age, like a wicked woman!"

On the fifth of February, her name-day, Agafya Mikhailovna received a telegram of congratulation from Stakhovitch.

When my father heard of it, he said jokingly to Agafya Mikhailovna:

"Aren't you ashamed that a man had to trudge two miles through the frost at night all for the sake of your telegram?"

"Trudge, trudge? Angels bore him on their wings. Trudge, indeed! You get three telegrams from an outlandish Jew woman," she growled, "and telegrams every day about your Golokhvotika. Never a trudge then; but I get name-day greetings, and it's trudge!"

And one could not but acknowledge that she was right. This telegram, the only one in the whole year that was addressed to the kennels, by the pleasure it gave Agafya Mikhailovna was far more important of course than this news or the about a ball given in Moscow in honor of a Jewish banker's daughter, or about Olga Andreyevna Golokvastovy's arrival at Yasnaya.

Agafya Mikhailovna died at the beginning of the nineties. There were no more hounds or sporting dogs at Yasnaya then, but till the end of her days she gave shelter to a motley collection of mongrels, and tended and fed them.

THE HOME OF THE TOLSTOYS

I CAN remember the house at Yasnaya Polyana in the condition it was in the first years after my father's marriage.

It was one of the two-storied wings of the old mansion-house of the Princes Volkonsky, which my father had sold for pulling down when he was still a bachelor.

From what my father has told me, I know that the house in which he was born and spent his youth was a three-storied building with thirty-six rooms. On the spot where it stood, between the two wings, the remains of the old stone foundation are still visible in the form of trenches filled with rubble, and the site is covered with big sixty-year-old trees that my father himself planted.

When any one asked my father where he was born, he used to point to a tall larch which grew on the site of the old foundations.

"Up there where the top of that larch waves," he used to say; "that's where my mother's room was, where I was born on a leather sofa."

My father seldom spoke of his mother, but when he did, it was delightful to hear him, because the mention of her awoke an unusual strain of gentleness and tenderness in him. There was such a ring of respectful affection, so much reverence for her memory, in his words, that we all looked on her as a sort of saint.

My father remembered his father well, because he was already nine years old when he died. He loved him, too, and always spoke of him reverently; but one always felt that his mother's memory, although he had never known her, was dearer to him, and his love for her far greater than for his father.

Even to this day I do not exactly know the story of the sale of the old house. My father never liked talking about it, and for that reason I could never make up my mind to ask him the details of the transaction. I only know that the house was sold for five thousand paper rubles 3 by one of his relatives, who had charge of his affairs by power of attorney when he was in the Caucasus.

It was said to have been done in order to pay off my father's gambling debts. That was quite true.

My father himself told me that at one time he was a great card-player, that he lost large sums of money, and that his financial affairs were considerably embarrassed.

The only thing about which I am in doubt is whether it was with my father's knowledge or by his directions that the house was sold, or whether the relative in question did not exceed his instructions and decide on the sale of his own initiative.

My father cherished his parents' memory to such an extent, and had such a warm affection for everything relating to his own childhood, that it is hard to believe that he would have raised his hand against the house in which he had been born and brought up and in which his mother had spent her whole life.

Knowing my father as I do, I think it is highly possible that he wrote to his relative from the Caucasus, "Sell something," not in the least expecting that he would sell the house, and that he afterward took the blame for it on himself. Is that not the reason why he was always so unwilling to talk about it?

In 1871, when I was five years old, the zala 4 and study were built on the house.

The walls of the zala were hung with old portraits of ancestors. They were rather alarming, and I was afraid of them at first; but we got used to them after a time, and I grew fond of one of them, of my great-grandfather, Ilya Andreyevitch Tolstoy, because I was told that I was like him.

Beside him hung the portrait of another great-grandfather, Prince Nikolai Sergeyevitch Volkonsky, my grandmother's father, with thick, black eyebrows, a gray wig, and a red kaftan. 5

This Volkonsky built all the buildings of Yasnaya Polyana. He was a model squire, intelligent and proud, and enjoyed the great respect of all the neighborhood.

On the ground floor, under the drawing-room, next to the entrance-hall, my father built his study. He had a semi-circular niche made in the wall, and stood a marble bust of his favorite dead brother Nikolai in it. This bust was made abroad from a death-mask, and my father told us that it was very like, because it was done by a good sculptor, according to his own directions.

He had a kind and rather plaintive face. The hair was brushed smooth like a child's, with the parting on one side. He had no beard or mustache, and his head was white and very, very clean. My father's study was divided in two by a partition of big bookshelves, containing a multitude of all sorts of books. In order to support them, the shelves were connected by big wooden beams, and between them was a thin birch-wood door, behind which stood my father's writing-table and his old-fashioned semicircular arm-chair.

There are portraits of Dickens and Schopenhauer and Fet 6 as a young man on the walls, too, and the well-known group of writers of the Sovremennik 7 circle in 1856, with Turgenieff, Ostrovsky, Gontcharof, Grigorovitch, Druzhinin, and my father, quite young still, without a beard, and in uniform.

My father used to come out of his bedroom of a morning—it was in a corner on the top floor—in his dressing-gown, with his beard uncombed and tumbled together, and go down to dress.

Soon after he would issue from his study fresh and vigorous, in a gray smock-frock, and would go up into the zala for breakfast. That was our dejeuner.

When there was nobody staying in the house, he would not stop long in the drawing-room, but would take his tumbler of tea and carry it off to his study with him.

But if there were friends and guests with us, he would get into conversation, become interested, and could not tear himself away.

At last he would go off to his work, and we would disperse, in winter to the different school-rooms, in summer to the croquet-lawn or somewhere about the garden. My mother would settle down in the drawing-room to make some garment for the babies, or to copy out something she had not finished overnight; and till three or four in the afternoon silence would reign in the house.

Then my father would come out of his study and go off for his afternoon's exercise. Sometimes he would take a dog and a gun, sometimes ride, and sometimes merely go for a walk to the imperial wood.

At five the big bell that hung on the broken bough of an old elm-tree in front of the house would ring and we would all run to wash our hands and collect for dinner.

He was very hungry, and ate voraciously of whatever turned up. My mother would try to stop him, would tell him not to waste all his appetite on kasha, because there were chops and vegetables to follow. "You'll have a bad liver again," she would say; but he would pay no attention to her, and would ask for more and more, until his hunger was completely satisfied. Then he would tell us all about his walk, where he put up a covey of black game, what new paths he discovered in the imperial wood beyond Kudeyarof Well, or, if he rode, how the young horse he was breaking in began to understand the reins and the pressure of the leg. All this he would relate in the most vivid and entertaining way, so that the time passed gaily and animatedly.

After dinner he would go back to his room to read, and at eight we had tea, and the best hours of the day began—the evening hours, when everybody gathered in the zala. The grown-ups talked or read aloud or played the piano, and we either listened to them or had some jolly game of our own, and in anxious fear awaited the moment when the English grandfather-clock on the landing would give a click and a buzz, and slowly and clearly ring out ten.

Perhaps mama would not notice? She was in the sitting-room, making a copy.

"Come, children, bedtime! Say good night," she would call.

"In a minute, Mama; just five minutes."

"Run along; it's high time; or there will be no getting you up in the morning to do your lessons."

We would say a lingering good night, on the lookout for any chance for delay, and at last would go down-stairs through the arches, annoyed at the thought that we were children still and had to go to bed while the grown-ups could stay up as long as ever they liked.

A JOURNEY TO THE STEPPES

WHEN I was still a child and had not yet read "War and Peace," I was told that NATASHA ROSTOF was Aunt Tanya. When my father was asked whether that was true, and whether DMITRY ROSTOF was such and such a person and LEVIN such and such another, he never gave a definite answer, and one could not but feel that he disliked such questions and was rather offended by them.

In those remote days about which I am talking, my father was very keen about the management of his estate, and devoted a lot of energy to it. I can remember his planting the huge apple orchard at Yasnaya and several hundred acres of birch and pine forest, and at the beginning of the seventies, for a number of years, he was interested in buying up land cheap in the province of Samara, and breeding droves of steppe horses and flocks of sheep.

I still have pretty clear, though rather fragmentary and inconsequent, recollections of our three summer excursions to the steppes of Samara.

My father had already been there before his marriage in 1862, and afterward by the advice of Dr. Zakharyin, who attended him. He took the kumiss-cure in 1871 and 1872, and at last, in 1873, the whole family went there.

At that time my father had bought several hundred acres of cheap Bashkir lands in the district of Buzuluk, and we went to stay on our new property at a khutor, or farm.

In Samara we lived on the farm in a tumble-down wooden house, and beside us, in the steppe, were erected two felt kibitkas, or Tatar frame tents, in which our Bashkir, Muhammed Shah Romanytch, lived with his wives.

Morning and evening they used to tie the mares up outside the kibitkas, where they were milked by veiled women, who then hid themselves from the sight of the men behind a brilliant chintz curtain, and made the kumiss.

The kumiss was bitter and very nasty, but my father and my uncle Stephen Behrs were very fond of it, and drank it in large quantities.

When we boys began to get big, we had at first a German tutor for two or three years, Fyodor Fyodorovitch Kaufmann.

I cannot say that we were particularly fond of him. He was rather rough, and even we children were struck by his German stupidity. His redeeming feature was that he was a devoted sportsman. Every morning he used to jerk the blankets off us and shout, "Auf, Kinder! auf!" and during the daytime plagued us with German calligraphy.

OUTDOOR SPORTS

THE chief passion of my childhood was riding. I well remember the time when my father used to put me in the saddle in front of him and we would ride out to bathe in the Voronka. I have several interesting recollections connected with these rides.

One day as we were going to bathe, papa turned round and said to me:

"Do you know, Ilyusha, I am very pleased with myself to-day. I have been bothered with her for three whole days, and could not manage to make her go into the house; try as I would, it was impossible. It never would come right. But to-day I remembered that there is a mirror in every hall, and that every lady wears a bonnet.

"As soon as I remembered that, she went where I wanted her to, and did everything she had to. You would think a bonnet is a small affair, but everything depended on that bonnet."

As I recall this conversation, I feel sure that my father was talking about that scene in "Anna Karenina" where ANNA went to see her son.

Although in the final form of the novel nothing is said in this scene either about a bonnet or a mirror,—nothing is mentioned but a thick black veil,—still, I imagine that in its original form, when he was working on the passage, my father may have brought Anna up to the mirror, and made her straighten her bonnet or take it off.

I can remember the interest with which he told me this, and it now seems strange that he should have talked about such subtle artistic experiences to a boy of seven who was hardly capable of understanding him at the time. However, that was often the case with him.

I once heard from him a very interesting description of what a writer needs for his work:

"You cannot imagine how important one's mood is," he said. "Sometimes you get up in the morning, fresh and vigorous, with your head clear, and you begin to write. Everything is sensible and consistent. You read it over next day, and have to throw the whole thing away, because, good as it is, it misses the main thing. There is no imagination in it, no subtlety, none of the necessary something, none of that only just without which all your cleverness is worth nothing. Another day you get up after a bad night, with your nerves all on edge, and you think, 'To-day I shall write well, at any rate.' And as a matter of fact, what you write is beautiful, picturesque, with any amount of imagination. You look it through again; it is no good, because it is written stupidly. There is plenty of color, but not enough intelligence.

"One's writing is good only when the intelligence and the imagination are in equilibrium. As soon as one of them overbalances the other, it's all up; you may as well throw it away and begin afresh."

As a matter of fact, there was no end to the rewriting in my father's works. His industry in this particular was truly marvelous.

We were always devoted to sport from our earliest childhood. I can remember as well as I remember myself my father's favorite dog in those days, an Irish setter called Dora. They would bring round the cart, with a very quiet horse between the shafts, and we would drive out to the marsh, to Degatna or to Malakhov. My father and sometimes my mother or a coachman sat on the seat, while I and Dora lay on the floor.

When we got to the marsh, my father used to get out, stand his gun on the ground, and, holding it with his left hand, load it.

Dora meanwhile fidgeted about, whining impatiently and wagging her thick tail.

While my father splashed through the marsh, we drove round the bank somewhat behind him, and eagerly followed the ranging of the dog, the getting up of the snipe, and the shooting. My father sometimes shot fairly well, though he often lost his head, and missed frantically.

But our favorite sport was coursing with greyhounds. What a pleasure it was when the footman Sergei Petrovitch came in and woke us up before dawn, with a candle in his hand!

We jumped up full of energy and happiness, trembling all over in the morning cold; threw on our clothes as quickly as we could, and ran out into the zala, where the samovar was boiling and papa was waiting for us.

Sometimes mama came in in her dressing-gown, and made us put on all sorts of extra woolen stockings, and sweaters and gloves.

"What are you going to wear, Lyovotchka?" she would say to papa. "It's very cold to-day, and there is a wind. Only the Kuzminsky overcoat again today? You must put on something underneath, if only for my sake."

Papa would make a face, but give in at last, and buckle on his short gray overcoat under the other and sally forth. It would then be growing light. Our horses were brought round, we got on, and rode first to "the other house," or to the kennels to get the dogs.

Agafya Mikhailovna would be anxiously waiting us on the steps. Despite the coldness of the morning, she would be bareheaded and lightly clad, with her black jacket open, showing her withered, old bosom. She carried the dog-collars in her lean, knotted hands.

"Have you gone and fed them again?" asks my father, severely, looking at the dogs' bulging stomachs.

"Fed them? Not a bit; only just a crust of bread apiece."

"Then what are they licking their chops for?"

"There was a bit of yesterday's oatmeal left over."

"I thought as much! All the hares will get away again. It really is too bad! Do you do it to spite me?"

"You can't have the dogs running all day on empty stomachs, Lyoff Nikolaievich," she grunted, going angrily to put on the dogs' collars.

At last the dogs were got together, some of them on leashes, others running free; and we would ride out at a brisk trot past Bitter Wells and the grove into the open country.

My father would give the word of command, "Line out!" and point out the direction in which we were to go, and we spread out over the stubble fields and meadows, whistling and winding about along the lee side of the steep balks, 8 beating all the bushes with our hunting-crops, and gazing keenly at every spot or mark on the earth.

Something white would appear ahead. We stared hard at it, gathered up the reins, examined the leash, scarcely believing the good luck of having come on a hare at last. Then riding up closer and closer, with our eyes on the white thing, it would turn out to be not a hare at all, but a horse's skull. How annoying!

We would look at papa and Seryozha, thinking, "I wonder if they saw that I took that skull for a hare." But papa would be sitting keen and alert on his English saddle, with the wooden stirrups, smoking a cigarette, while Seryozha would perhaps have got his leash entangled and could not get it straight.

"Thank heaven!" we would exclaim, "nobody saw me! What a fool I should have felt!" So we would ride on.

The horse's even pace would begin to rock us to sleep, feeling rather bored at nothing getting up; when all of a sudden, just at the moment we least expected it, right in front of us, twenty paces away, would jump up a gray hare as if from the bowels of the earth.

The dogs had seen it before we had, and had started forward already in full pursuit. We began to bawl, "Tally-ho! tally-ho!" like madmen, flogging our horses with all our might, and flying after them.

The dogs would come up with the hare, turn it, then turn it again, the young and fiery Sultan and Darling running over it, catching up again, and running over again; and at last the old and experienced Winger, who had been galloping on one side all the time, would seize her opportunity, and spring in. The hare would give a helpless cry like a baby, and the dogs, burying their fangs in it, in a star-shaped group, would begin to tug in different directions.

"Let go! Let go!"

We would come galloping up, finish off the hare, and give the dogs the tracks, 9 tearing them off toe by toe, and throwing them to our favorites, who would catch them in the air. Then papa would teach us how to strap the hare on the back of the saddle.

After the run we would all be in better spirits, and get to better places near Yasenki and Retinka. Gray hares would get up oftener. Each of us would have his spoils in the saddle-straps now, and we would begin to hope for a fox.

Not many foxes would turn up. If they did, it was generally Tumashka, who was old and staid, who distinguished himself. He was sick of hares, and made no great effort to run after them; but with a fox he would gallop at full speed, and it was almost always he who killed.

It would be late, often dark, when we got back home.

"ANNA KARENINA"

I REMEMBER my father writing his alphabet and reading-book in 1871 and 1872, but I cannot at all remember his beginning "Anna Karenina." I probably knew nothing about it at the time. What did it matter to a boy of seven what his father was writing? It was only later, when one kept hearing the name again and again, and bundles of proofs kept arriving, and were sent off almost every day, that I understood that "Anna Karenina" was the name of the novel on which my father and mother were both at work.

My mother's work seemed much harder than my father's, because we actually saw her at it, and she worked much longer hours than he did. She used to sit in the sitting-room off the zala, at her little writing-table, and spend all her free time writing.

Leaning over the manuscript and trying to decipher my father's scrawl with her short-sighted eyes, she used to spend whole evenings over it, and often sat up late at night after everybody else had gone to bed. Sometimes, when anything was written quite illegibly, she would go to my father's study and ask him what it meant. But this was very rare, because my mother did not like to disturb him.

When it happened, my father used to take the manuscript in his hand, and ask with some annoyance, "What on earth is the difficulty?" and would begin to read it out aloud. When he came to the difficult place he would mumble and hesitate, and sometimes had the greatest difficulty in making out, or, rather, in guessing, what he had written. He had a very bad handwriting, and a terrible habit of writing in whole sentences between the lines, or in the corners of the page, or sometimes right across it.

My mother often discovered gross grammatical errors, and pointed them out to my father, and corrected them.

When "Anna Karenina" began to come out in the "Russky Vyestnik," 10 long galley-proofs were posted to my father, and he looked them through and corrected them.

At first the margins would be marked with the ordinary typographical signs, letters omitted, marks of punctuation, etc.; then individual words would be changed, and then whole sentences, till in the end the proof-sheet would be reduced to a mass of patches quite black in places, and it was quite impossible to send it back as it stood, because no one but my mother could make head or tail of the tangle of conventional signs, transpositions, and erasures.

My mother would sit up all night copying the whole thing out afresh.

In the morning there would lie the pages on her table, neatly piled together, covered all over with her fine, clear handwriting, and everything ready so that when "Lyovotchka" got up he could send the proof-sheets off by post.

My father carried them off to his study to have "just one last look," and by the evening it would be just as bad again, the whole thing having been rewritten and messed up.

"Sonya my dear, I am very sorry, but I've spoiled all your work again; I promise I won't do it any more," he would say, showing her the passages he had inked over with a guilty air. "We'll send them off to-morrow without fail." But this to-morrow was often put off day by day for weeks or months together.

"There's just one bit I want to look through again," my father would say; but he would get carried away and recast the whole thing afresh.

There were even occasions when, after posting the proofs, he would remember some particular words next day, and correct them by telegraph. Several times, in consequence of these rewritings, the printing of the novel in the "Russky Vyestnik" was interrupted, and sometimes it did not come out for months together.

In the last part of "Anna Karenina" my father, in describing the end of VRONSKY'S career, showed his disapproval of the volunteer movement and the Panslavonic committees, and this led to a quarrel with Katkof.

I can remember how angry my father was when Katkof refused to print those chapters as they stood, and asked him either to leave out part of them or to soften them down, and finally returned the manuscript, and printed a short note in his paper to say that after the death of the heroine the novel was strictly speaking at an end; but that the author had added an epilogue of two printed sheets, in which he related such and such facts, and he would very likely "develop these chapters for the separate edition of his novel."

In concluding, I wish to say a few words about my father's own opinion of "Anna Karenina."

In 1875 he wrote to N. N. Strakhof:

"I must confess that I was delighted by the success of the last piece of 'Anna Karenina.' I had by no means expected it, and to tell you the truth, I am surprised that people are so pleased with such ordinary and EMPTY stuff."

The same year he wrote to Fet:

"It is two months since I have defiled my hands with ink or my heart with thoughts. But now I am setting to work again on my TEDIOUS, VULGAR 'ANNA KARENINA,' with only one wish, to clear it out of the way as soon as possible and give myself leisure for other occupations, but not schoolmastering, which I am fond of, but wish to give up; it takes up too much time."

In 1878, when the novel was nearing its end, he wrote again to Strakhof:

"I am frightened by the feeling that I am getting into my summer mood again. I LOATHE what I have written. The proof-sheets for the April number [of "Anna Karenina" in the "Russky Vyestnik"] now lie on my table, and I am afraid that I have not the heart to correct them. EVERYTHING in them is BEASTLY, and the whole thing ought to be rewritten,—all that has been printed, too,—scrapped and melted down, thrown away, renounced. I ought to say, 'I am sorry; I will not do it any more,' and try to write something fresh instead of all this incoherent, neither-fish-nor-flesh-nor-fowlish stuff."

That was how my father felt toward his novel while he was writing it. Afterward I often heard him say much harsher things about it.

"What difficulty is there in writing about how an officer fell in love with a married woman?" he used to say. "There's no difficulty in it, and above all no good in it."

I am quite convinced that if my father could have done so, he long ago would have destroyed this novel, which he never liked and always wanted to disown.

(To be continued)

REMINISCENCES OF TOLSTOY (Part II.)

BY HIS SON, COUNT ILYA TOLSTOY

TRANSLATED BY GEORGE CALDERON

IN the summer, when both families were together at Yasnaya, our own and the Kuzminsky's, when both the house and the annex were full of the family and their guests, we used our letter-box.

It originated long before, when I was still small and had only just learned to write, and it continued with intervals till the middle of the eighties.

It hung on the landing at the top of the stairs beside the grandfather's clock; and every one dropped his compositions into it, the verses, articles, or stories that he had written on topical subjects in the course of the week.

On Sundays we would all collect at the round table in the zala, the box would be solemnly opened, and one of the grown-ups, often my father himself, would read the contents aloud.

All the papers were unsigned, and it was a point of honor not to peep at the handwriting; but, despite this, we almost always guessed the author, either by the style, by his self-consciousness, or else by the strained indifference of his expression.

When I was a boy, and for the first time wrote a set of French verses for the letter-box, I was so shy when they were read that I hid under the table, and sat there the whole evening until I was pulled out by force.

For a long time after, I wrote no more, and was always fonder of hearing other people's compositions read than my own.

All the events of our life at Yasnaya Polyana found their echo in one way or another in the letter-box, and no one was spared, not even the grown-ups.

All our secrets, all our love-affairs, all the incidents of our complicated life were revealed in the letter-box, and both household and visitors were good-humoredly made fun of.

Unfortunately, much of the correspondence has been lost, but bits of it have been preserved by some of us in copies or in memory. I cannot recall everything interesting that there was in it, but here are a few of the more interesting things from the period of the eighties.

THE LETTER-BOX

THE old fogy continues his questions. Why, when women or old men enter the room, does every well-bred person not only offer them a seat, but give them up his own?

Why do they make Ushakof or some Servian officer who comes to pay a visit necessarily stay to tea or dinner?

Why is it considered wrong to let an older person or a woman help you on with your overcoat?

And why are all these charming rules considered obligatory toward others, when every day ordinary people come, and we not only do not ask them to sit down or to stop to dinner or spend the night or render them any service, but would look on it as the height of impropriety?

Where do those people end to whom we are under these obligations? By what characteristics are the one sort distinguished from the others? And are not all these rules of politeness bad, if they do not extend to all sorts of people? And is not what we call politeness an illusion, and a very ugly illusion?

LYOFF TOLSTOY.

Question: Which is the most "beastly plague," a cattle-plague case for a farmer, or the ablative case for a school-boy?

LYOFF TOLSTOY.

Answers are requested to the following questions:

Why do Ustyusha, Masha, Alyona, Peter, etc., have to bake, boil, sweep, empty slops, wait at table, while the gentry have only to eat, gobble, quarrel, make slops, and eat again?

LYOFF TOLSTOY.

My Aunt Tanya, when she was in a bad temper because the coffee-pot had been spilt or because she had been beaten at croquet, was in the habit of sending every one to the devil. My father wrote the following story, "Susoitchik," about it.

The devil, not the chief devil, but one of the rank and file, the one charged with the management of social affairs, Susoitchik by name, was greatly perturbed on the 6th of August, 1884. From the early morning onward, people kept arriving who had been sent him by Tatyana Kuzminsky.

The first to arrive was Alexander Mikhailovitch Kuzminsky; the second was Misha Islavin; the third was Vyatcheslaf; the fourth was Seryozha Tolstoy, and last of all came old Lyoff Tolstoy, senior, accompanied by Prince Urusof. The first visitor, Alexander Mikhailovitch, caused Susoitchik no surprise, as he often paid Susoitchik visits in obedience to the behests of his wife.

"What, has your wife sent you again?"

"Yes," replied the presiding judge of the district-court, shyly, not knowing what explanation he could give of the cause of his visit.

"You come here very often. What do you want?"

"Oh, nothing in particular; she just sent her compliments," murmured Alexander Mikhailovitch, departing from the exact truth with some effort.

"Very good, very good; come whenever you like; she is one of my best workers."

Before Susoitchik had time to show the judge out, in came all the children, laughing and jostling, and hiding one behind the other.

"What brought you here, youngsters? Did my little Tanyitchka send you? That's right; no harm in coming. Give my compliments to Tanya, and tell her that I am always at her service. Come whenever you like. Old Susoitchik may be of use to you."

No sooner had the young folk made their bow than old Lyoff Tolstoy appeared with Prince Urusof.

"Aha! so it's the old boy! Many thanks to Tanyitchka. It's a long time since I have seen you, old chap. Well and hearty? And what can I do for you?"

Lyoff Tolstoy shuffled about, rather abashed.

Prince Urusof, mindful of the etiquette of diplomatic receptions, stepped forward and explained Tolstoy's appearance by his wish to make acquaintance with Tatyana Andreyevna's oldest and most faithful friend.

"Les amis des nos amis sont nos amis."

"Ha! ha! ha! quite so!" said Susoitchik. "I must reward her for today's work. Be so kind, Prince, as to hand her the marks of my good-will."

And he handed over the insignia of an order in a morocco case. The insignia consisted of a necklace of imp's tails to be worn about the throat, and two toads, one to be worn on the bosom and the other on the bustle.

LYOFF TOLSTOY, SENIOR.

SERGEI NIKOLAYEVITCH TOLSTOY

I CAN remember my Uncle Seryozha (Sergei) from my earliest childhood. He lived at Pirogovo, twenty miles from Yasnaya, and visited us often.

As a young man he was very handsome. He had the same features as my father, but he was slenderer and more aristocratic-looking. He had the same oval face, the same nose, the same intelligent gray eyes, and the same thick, overhanging eyebrows. The only difference between his face and my father's was defined by the fact that in those distant days, when my father cared for his personal appearance, he was always worrying about his ugliness, while Uncle Seryozha was considered, and really was, a very handsome man.

This is what my father says about Uncle Seryozha in his fragmentary reminiscences:

"I and Nitenka 11 were chums, Nikolenka I revered, but Seryozha I admired enthusiastically and imitated; I loved him and wished to be he.

"I admired his handsome exterior, his singing,—he was always a singer,—his drawing, his gaiety, and above all, however strange a thing it may seem to say, the directness of his egoism. 12

"I always remembered myself, was aware of myself, always divined rightly or wrongly what others thought about me and felt toward me; and this spoiled the joy of life for me. This was probably the reason why I particularly delighted in the opposite of this in other people; namely, directness of egoism. That is what I especially loved in Seryozha, though the word 'loved' is inexact.

"I loved Nikolenka, but I admired Seryozha as something alien and incomprehensible to me. It was a human life very beautiful, but completely incomprehensible to me, mysterious, and therefore especially attractive.

"He died only a few days ago, and while he was ill and while he was dying he was just as inscrutable and just as dear to me as he had been in the distant days of our childhood.

"In these latter days, in our old age, he was fonder of me, valued my attachment more, was prouder of me, wanted to agree with me, but could not, and remained just the same as he had always been; namely, something quite apart, only himself, handsome, aristocratic, proud, and, above all, truthful and sincere to a degree that I never met in any other man.

"He was what he was; he concealed nothing, and did not wish to appear anything different."

Uncle Seryozha never treated children affectionately; on the contrary, he seemed to put up with us rather than to like us. But we always treated him with particular reverence. The result, as I can see now, partly of his aristocratic appearance, but chiefly because of the fact that he called my father "Lyovotchka" and treated him just as my father treated us.

He was not only not in the least afraid of him, but was always teasing him, and argued with him like an elder person with a younger. We were quite alive to this.

Of course every one knew that there were no faster dogs in the world than our black-and-white Darling and her daughter Wizard. Not a hare could get away from them. But Uncle Seryozha said that the gray hares about us were sluggish creatures, not at all the same thing as steppe hares, and neither Darling nor Wizard would get near a steppe hare.

We listened with open mouths, and did not know which to believe, papa or Uncle Seryozha.

Uncle Seryozha went out coursing with us one day. A number of gray hares were run down, not one, getting away; Uncle Seryozha expressed no surprise, but still maintained that the only reason was because they were a poor lot of hares. We could not tell whether he was right or wrong.

Perhaps, after all, he was right, for he was more of a sportsman than papa and had run down ever so many wolves, while we had never known papa run any wolves down.

Afterward papa kept dogs only because there was Agafya Mikhailovna to be thought of, and Uncle Seryozha gave up sport because it was impossible to keep dogs.

"Since the emancipation of the peasants," he said, "sport is out of the question; there are no huntsmen to be had, and the peasants turn out with sticks and drive the sportsmen off the fields. What is there left to do nowadays? Country life has become impossible."

With all his good breeding and sincerity, Uncle Seryozha never concealed any characteristic but one; with the utmost shyness he concealed the tenderness of his affections, and if it ever forced itself into the light, it was only in exceptional circumstances and that against his will.

He displayed with peculiar clearness a family characteristic which was partly shared by my father, namely, an extraordinary restraint in the expression of affection, which was often concealed under the mask of indifference and sometimes even of unexpected harshness. In the matter of wit and sarcasm, on the other hand, he was strikingly original.

At one period he spent several winters in succession with his family in Moscow. One time, after a historic concert given by Anton Rubinstein, at which Uncle Seryozha and his daughter had been, he came to take tea with us in Weavers' Row.13

My father asked him how he had liked the concert.

"Do you remember Himbut, Lyovotchka? Lieutenant Himbut, who was forester near Yasnaya? I once asked him what was the happiest moment of his life. Do you know what he answered?

"'When I was in the cadet corps,' he said, 'they used to take down my breeches now and again and lay me across a bench and flog me. They flogged and they flogged; when they stopped, that was the happiest moment of my life.' Well, it was only during the entr'actes, when Rubinstein stopped playing, that I really enjoyed myself."

He did not always spare my father.

Once when I was out shooting with a setter near Pirogovo, I drove in to Uncle Seryozha's to stop the night.

I do not remember apropos of what, but Uncle Seryozha averred that Lyovotchka was proud. He said:

"He is always preaching humility and non-resistance, but he is proud himself.

"Nashenka's 14 sister had a footman called Forna. When he got drunk, he used to get under the staircase, tuck in his legs, and lie down. One day they came and told him that the countess was calling him. 'She can come and find me if she wants me,' he answered.

"Lyovotchka is just the same. When Dolgoruky sent his chief secretary Istomin to ask him to come and have a talk with him about Syntayef, the sectarian, do you know what he answered?

"'Let him come here, if he wants me.' Isn't that just the same as Forna?

"No, Lyovotchka is very proud. Nothing would induce him to go, and he was quite right; but it's no good talking of humility."

During the last years of Sergei Nikolayevitch's life my father was particularly friendly and affectionate with him, and delighted in sharing his thoughts with him.

A. A. Fet in his reminiscences describes the character of all the three Tolstoy brothers with extraordinary perspicacity:

I am convinced that the fundamental type of all the three Tolstoy brothers was identical, just as the type of all maple-leaves is identical, despite the variety of their configurations. And if I set myself to develop the idea, I could show to what a degree all three brothers shared in that passionate enthusiasm without which it would have been impossible for one of them to turn into the poet Lyoff Tolstoy. The difference of their attitude to life was determined by the difference of the ways in which they turned their backs on their unfulfilled dreams. Nikolai quenched his ardor in skeptical derision, Lyoff renounced his unrealized dreams with silent reproach, and Sergei with morbid misanthropy. The greater the original store of love in such characters, the stronger, if only for a time, is their resemblance to Timon of Athens.

In the winter of 1901-02 my father was ill in the Crimea, and for a long time lay between life and death. Uncle Seryozha, who felt himself getting weaker, could not bring himself to leave Pirogovo, and in his own home followed anxiously the course of my father's illness by the letters which several members of our family wrote him, and by the bulletins in the newspapers.

When my father began to improve, I went back home, and on the way from the Crimea went to Pirogovo, in order to tell Uncle Seryozha personally about the course of the illness and about the present condition of my father's health. I remember how joyfully and gratefully he welcomed me.

"How glad I am that you came! Now tell me all about it. Who is with him? All of them? And who nurses him most? Do you go on duty in turn? And at night, too? He can't get out of bed. Ah, that's the worst thing of all!

"It will be my turn to die soon; a year sooner or later, what does it matter? But to lie helpless, a burden to every one, to have others doing everything for you, lifting you and helping you to sit up, that's what's so awful.

"And how does he endure it? Got used to it, you say? No; I cannot imagine having Vera to change my linen and wash me. Of course she would say that it's nothing to her, but for me it would be awful.

"And tell me, is he afraid to die? Does he say not? Very likely; he's a strong man, he may be able to conquer the fear of it. Yes, yes, perhaps he's not afraid; but still—

"You say he struggles with the feeling? Why, of course; what else can one do?

"I wanted to go and be with him; but I thought, how can I? I shall crack up myself, and then there will be two invalids instead of one.

"Yes, you have told me a great deal; every detail is interesting. It is not death that's so terrible, it's illness, helplessness, and, above all, the fear that you are a burden to others. That's awful, awful."

Uncle Seryozha died in 1904 of cancer in the face. This is what my aunt, Maria Nikolayevna,[15] the nun, told me about his death. Almost to the last day he was on his legs, and would not let any one nurse him. He was in full possession of his faculties and consciously prepared for death.

Besides his own family, the aged Maria Mikhailovna and her daughters, his sister, Maria Nikolayevna, who told me the story, was with him, too, and from hour to hour they expected the arrival of my father, for whom they had sent a messenger to Yasnaya. They were all troubled with the difficult question whether the dying man would want to receive the holy communion before he died.

Knowing Sergei Nikolayevitch's disbelief in the religion of the church, no one dared to mention the subject to him, and the unhappy Maria Mikhailovna hovered round his room, wringing her hands and praying.

They awaited my father's arrival impatiently, but were secretly afraid of his influence on his brother, and hoped against hope that Sergei Nikolayevitch would send for the priest before his arrival.

"Imagine our surprise and delight," said Maria Tolstoy, "when Lyovotchka came out of his room and told Maria Mikhailovna that

Seryozha wanted a priest sent for. I do not know what they had been talking about, but when Seryozha said that he wished to take the communion, Lyovotchka answered that he was quite right, and at once came and told us what he wanted."

My father stayed about a week at Pirogovo, and left two days before my uncle died.

When he received a telegram to say he was worse, he drove over again, but arrived too late; he was no longer living. He carried his body out from the house with his own hands, and himself bore it to the churchyard.

When he got back to Yasnaya he spoke with touching affection of his parting with this "inscrutable and beloved" brother, who was so strange and remote from him, but at the same time so near and so akin.

FET, STRAKHOF, GAY

"WHAT'S this saber doing here?" asked a young guardsman, Lieutenant Afanasyi Afanasyevitch Fet, of the footman one day as he entered the hall of Ivan Sergeyevitch Turgenieff's flat in St. Petersburg in the middle of the fifties.

"It is Count Tolstoy's saber; he is asleep in the drawing-room. And Ivan Sergeyevitch is in his study having breakfast," replied Zalchar.

"During the hour I spent with Turgenieff," says Fet, in his reminiscences, "we talked in low voices, for fear of waking the count, who was asleep on the other side of the door."

"He's like that all the time," said Turgenieff, smiling; "ever since he got back from his battery at Sebastopol, 16 and came to stay here, he has been going the pace. Orgies, Gipsies, and gambling all night long, and then sleeps like a dead man till two o'clock in the afternoon. I did my best to stop him, but have given it up as a bad job.

"It was in this visit to St. Petersburg that I and Tolstoy became acquainted, but the acquaintance was of a purely formal character, as I had not yet seen a line of his writings, and had never heard of his name in literature, except that Turgenieff mentioned his 'Stories of Childhood.'"

Soon after this my father came to know Fet intimately, and they struck up a firm and lasting friendship, and established a correspondence which lasted almost till Fet's death.

It was only during the last years of Fet's life, when my father was entirely absorbed in his new ideas, which were so at variance with Afanasyi Afanasyevitch's whole philosophy of life, that they became estranged and met more rarely.

It was at Fet's, at Stepanovka, that my father and Turgenieff quarreled.

Before the railway was made, when people still had to drive, Fet, on his way into Moscow, always used to turn in at Yasnaya Polyana to see my father, and these visits became an established custom. Afterward, when the railway was made and my father was already married, Afanasyi Afanasyevitch still never passed our house without coming in, and if he did, my father used to write him a letter of earnest reproaches, and he used to apologize as if he had been guilty of some fault. In those distant times of which I am speaking my father was bound to Fet by a common interest in agriculture as well as literature.

Some of my father's letters of the sixties are curious in this respect.

For instance, in 1860, he wrote a long dissertation on Turgenieff's novel "On the Eve," which had just come out, and at the end added a postscript: "What is the price of a set of the best quality of veterinary instruments? And what is the price of a set of lancets and bleeding-cups for human use?"

In another letter there is a postscript:

"When you are next in Oryol, buy me six-hundred weight of various ropes, reins, and traces," and on the same page: "'Tender art thou,' and the whole thing is charming. You have never done anything better; it is all charming." The quotation is from Fet's poem:

The lingering clouds' last throng flies over us.

But it was not only community of interests that brought my father and Afanasyi Afanasyevitch together. The reason of their intimacy lay in the fact that, as my father expressed it, they "thought alike with their heart's mind."

I also remember Nikolai Nikolayevitch Strakhof's visits. He was a remarkably quiet and modest man. He appeared at Yasnaya Polyana in the beginning of the seventies, and from that time on came and stayed with us almost every summer till he died.

He had big, gray eyes, wide open, as if in astonishment; a long beard with a touch of gray in it; and when he spoke, at the end of every sentence he gave a shy laugh.

When he addressed my father, he always said "Lef Nikolayevitch" instead of Lyoff Nikolaievich, like other people.

He always stayed down-stairs in my father's study, and spent his whole day there reading or writing, with a thick cigarette, which he rolled himself, in his mouth.

Strakhof and my father came together originally on a purely business footing. When the first part of my father's "Alphabet and Reading-Book" was printed, Strakhof had charge of the proof-reading. This led to a correspondence between him and my father, of a business character at first, later developing into a philosophical and friendly one. While he was writing "Anna Karenina," my father set great store by his opinion and valued his critical instinct very highly.

"It is enough for me that that is your opinion," he writes in a letter of 1872, probably apropos of the "Alphabet."

In 1876, apropos of "Anna Karenina" this time, my father wrote:

"You ask me whether you have understood my novel aright, and what I think of your opinion. Of course you understood it aright. Of course I am overjoyed at your understanding of it; but it does not follow that everybody will understand it as you do."

But it was not only his critical work that drew my father to Strakhof. He disliked critics on the whole and used to say that the only people who took to criticism were those who had no creative faculty of their own. "The stupid ones judge the clever ones," he said of professional critics. What he valued most in Strakhof was the profound and penetrating thinker. He was a "real friend" of my father's,—my father himself so described him,—and I recall his memory with deep affection and respect.

At last I have come to the memory of the man who was nearer in spirit to my father than any other human being, namely, Nikolai Nikolayevitch Gay. Grandfather Gay, as we called him, made my father's acquaintance in 1882. While living on his farm in the Province of Tchernigoff, he chanced to read my father's pamphlet "On the Census," and finding a solution in it of the very questions which were troubling him at the time, without delay he started out and hurried into Moscow. I remember his first arrival, and I have always retained the impression that from the first words they exchanged he and my father understood each other, and found themselves speaking the same language.

Just like my father, Gay was at this time passing through a great spiritual crisis; and traveling almost the same road as my father in his search after truth, he had arrived at the study of the Gospel and a new understanding of it. My sister Tatyana wrote:

For the personality of Christ he entertained a passionate and tender affection, as if for a near and familiar friend whom he loved with all the strength of his soul. Often during heated arguments Nikolai Nikolayevitch would take the Gospel, which he always carried about with him, from his pocket, and read out some passage from it appropriate to the subject in hand. "This book contains everything that a man needs," he used to say on these occasions.

While reading the Gospel, he often looked up at the person he was talking to and went on reading without looking at the book. His face glowed at such moments with such inward joy that one could see how near and dear the words he was reading were to his heart.

He knew the whole Gospel almost by heart, but he said that every time he read it he enjoyed a new and genuine spiritual delight. He said that not only was everything intelligible to him in the Gospel, but that when he read it he seemed to be reading in his own soul, and felt himself capable of rising higher and higher toward God and merging himself in Him.

TURGENIEFF

I DO not mean to recount all the misunderstandings which existed between my father and Turgenieff, which ended in a complete breach between them in 1861. The actual external facts of that story are common property, and there is no need to repeat them. 17 According to general opinion, the quarrel between the two greatest writers of the day arose out of their literary rivalry.

It is my intention to show cause against this generally received opinion, and before I come to Turgenieff's visits to Yasnaya Polyana, I want to make as clear as I can the real reason of the perpetual discords between these two good-hearted people, who had a cordial affection for each other—discords which led in the end to an out-and-out quarrel and the exchange of mutual defiance.

As far as I know, my father never had any serious difference with any other human being during the whole course of his existence. And Turgenieff, in a letter to my father in 1865, wrote, "You are the only man with whom I have ever had misunderstandings."

Whenever my father related his quarrel with Ivan Sergeyevitch, he took all the blame on himself. Turgenieff, immediately after the quarrel, wrote a letter apologizing to my father, and never sought to justify his own part in it.

Why was it that, as Turgenieff himself put it, his "constellation" and my father's "moved in the ether with unquestioned enmity"?

This is what my sister Tatyana wrote on the subject in her article "Turgenieff," published in the supplement to the "Novoye Vremya," February 2, 1908:

All question of literary rivalry, it seems to me, is utterly beside the mark. Turgenieff, from the very outset of my father's literary career, acknowledged his enormous talents, and never thought of rivalry with him. From the moment when, as early as 1854, he wrote to Kolbasina, "If Heaven only grant Tolstoy life, I confidently hope that he will surprise us all," he never ceased to follow my father's work with interest, and always expressed his unbounded admiration of it.

"When this young wine has done fermenting," he wrote to Druzhenin in 1856, "the result will be a liquor worthy of the gods." In 1857 he wrote to Polonsky, "This man will go far, and leave deep traces behind him."

Nevertheless, somehow these two men never could "hit it off" together. When one reads Turgenieff's letters to my father, one sees that from the very beginning of their acquaintance misunderstandings were always arising, which they perpetually endeavored to smooth down or to forget, but which arose again after a time, sometimes in another form, necessitating new explanations and reconciliations.

In 1856 Turgenieff wrote to my father:

Your letter took some time reaching me, dear Lyoff Nikolaievich. Let me begin by saying that I am very grateful to you for sending it to me. I shall never cease to love you and to value your friendship, although, probably through my fault, each of us will long feel considerable awkwardness in the presence of the other.... I think that you yourself understand the reason of this awkwardness of which I speak. You are the only man with whom I have ever had misunderstandings.

This arises from the very fact that I have never been willing to confine myself to merely friendly relations with you. I have always wanted to go further and deeper than that; but I set about it clumsily. I irritated and upset you, and when I saw my mistake, I drew back too hastily, perhaps; and it was this which caused this "gulf" between us.

But this awkwardness is a mere physical impression, nothing more; and if when we meet again, you see the old "mischievous look in my eyes," believe me, the reason of it will not be that I am a bad man. I assure you that there is no need to look for any other explanation. Perhaps I may add, also, that I am much older than you, and I have traveled a different road.... Outside of our special, so-called "literary" interests, I am convinced, we have few points of contact. Your whole being stretches out hands toward the future; mine is built up in the past. For me to follow you is impossible. For you to follow me is equally out of the question. You are too far removed from me, and besides, you stand too firmly on your own legs to become any one's disciple. I can assure you that I never attributed any malice to you, never suspected you of any literary envy. I have often thought, if you will excuse the expression, that you were wanting in common sense, but never in goodness. You are too penetrating not to know that if either of us has cause to envy the other, it is certainly not you that has cause to envy me.

The following year he wrote a letter to my father which, it seems to me, is a key to the understanding of Turgenieff's attitude toward him:

You write that you are very glad you did not follow my advice and become a pure man of letters. I don't deny it; perhaps you are right. Still, batter my poor brains as I may, I cannot imagine what else you are if you are not a man of letters. A soldier? A squire? A philosopher? The founder of a new religious doctrine? A civil servant? A man of business?... Please resolve my difficulties, and tell me which of these suppositions is correct. I am joking, but I really do wish beyond all things to see you under way at last, with all sails set.

It seems to me that Turgenieff, as an artist, saw nothing in my father beyond his great literary talent, and was unwilling to allow him the right to be anything besides an artist and a writer. Any other line of activity on my father's part offended Turgenieff, as it were, and he was angry with my father because he did not follow his advice. He was much older than my father, 18 he did not hesitate to rank his own talent lower than my father's, and demanded only one thing of him, that he should devote all the energies of his life to his literary work. And, lo and behold! my father would have nothing to do with his magnanimity and humility, would not listen to his advice, but insisted on going the road which his own tastes and nature pointed out to him. Turgenieff's tastes and character were diametrically opposed to my father's. While opposition always inspired my father and lent him strength, it had just the opposite effect on Turgenieff.

Being wholly in agreement with my sister's views, I will merely supplement them with the words uttered by his brother, Nikolai Nikolayevitch, who said that "Turgenieff cannot reconcile himself to the idea that Lyovotchka is growing up and freeing himself from his tutelage."

As a matter of fact, when Turgenieff was already a famous writer, no one had ever heard of Tolstoy, and, as Fet expressed it, there was only "something said about his stories from 'Childhood.'"

I can imagine with what secret veneration a young writer, just beginning, must have regarded Turgenieff at that time, and all the more because Ivan Sergeyevitch was a great friend of my father's elder and beloved brother Nikolai.

I do not like to assert it positively, but it seems to me that just as Turgenieff was unwilling to confine himself to "merely friendly relations," so my father also felt too warmly toward Ivan Sergeyevitch, and that was the very reason why they could never meet without disagreeing and quarreling. In confirmation of what I say here is a passage from a letter written by V. Botkin, a close friend of my father's and of Ivan Sergeyevitch's, to A. A. Fet, written immediately after their quarrel:

I think that Tolstoy really has a passionately affectionate nature and he would like to love Turgenieff in the warmest way possible; but unfortunately his impulsive feeling encounters nothing but a kindly, good-natured indifference, and he can by no means reconcile himself to that.

Turgenieff himself said that when they first came to know each other my father dogged his heels "like a woman in love," and at one time he used to avoid him, because he was afraid of his spirit of opposition.

My father was perhaps irritated by the slightly patronizing tone which Turgenieff adopted from the very outset of their acquaintance; and Turgenieff was irritated by my father's "crankiness," which distracted him from "his proper metier, literature."

In 1870, before the date of the quarrel, Turgenieff wrote to Fet:

"Lyoff Tolstoy continues to play the crank. It was evidently written in his stars. When will he turn his last somersault and stand on his feet at last?"

Turgenieff was just the same about my father's "Confession," which he read not long before his death. Having promised to read it, "to try to understand it," and "not to lose my temper," he "started to write a long letter in answer to the 'Confession,' but never finished it... for fear of becoming disputatious."

In a letter to D. V. Grigorevitch he called the book, which was based, in his opinion, on false premises, "a denial of all live human life" and "a new sort of Nihilism."

It is evident that even then Turgenieff did not understand what a mastery my father's new philosophy of life had obtained over him, and he was inclined to attribute his enthusiasm along with the rest to the same perpetual "crankinesses" and "somersaults" to which he had formerly attributed his interest in school-teaching, agriculture, the publication of a paper, and so forth.

IVAN SERGEYEVITCH three times visited Yasnaya Polyana within my memory, in: August and September, 1878, and the third and last time at the beginning of May, 1880. I can remember all these visits, although it is quite possible that some details have escaped me.

I remember that when we expected Turgenieff on his first visit, it was a great occasion, and the most anxious and excited of all the household about it was my mother. She told us that my father had quarreled with Turgenieff and had once challenged him to a duel, and that he was now coming at my father's invitation to effect a reconciliation.

Turgenieff spent all the time sitting with my father, who during his visit put aside even his work, and once in the middle of the day my mother collected us all at a quite unusual hour in the drawing-room, where Ivan Sergeyevitch read us his story of "The Dog."

I can remember his tall, stalwart figure, his gray, silky, yellowish hair, his soft tread, rather waddling walk, and his piping voice, quite out of keeping with his majestic exterior. He had a chuckling kind of laugh, like a child's, and when he laughed his voice was more piping than ever.

In the evening, after dinner, we all gathered in the zala. At that time Uncle Seryozha, Prince Leonid Dmitryevitch Urusof, Vice-Governor of the Province of Tula; Uncle Sasha Behrs and his young wife, the handsome Georgian Patty; and the whole family of the Kuzminskys, were staying at Yasnaya.

Aunt Tanya was asked to sing. We listened with beating hearts, and waited to hear what Turgenieff, the famous connoisseur, would say about her singing. Of course he praised it, sincerely, I think. After the singing a quadrille was got up. All of a sudden, in the middle of the quadrille, Ivan Sergeyevitch, who was sitting at one side looking on, got up and took one of the ladies by the hand, and, putting his thumbs into the armholes of his waistcoat, danced a cancan according to the latest rules of Parisian art. Everyone roared with laughter, Turgenieff more than anybody.

After tea the "grown-ups" started some conversation, and a warm dispute arose among them. It was Prince Urusof who disputed most warmly, and "went for" Turgenieff.

Of Turgenieff's third visit I remember the woodcock shooting. This was on the second or third of May, 1880.

We all went out together beyond the Voronka, my father, my mother and all the children. My father gave Turgenieff the best place and posted himself one hundred and fifty paces away at the other end of the same glade.

My mother stood by Turgenieff, and we children lighted a bonfire not far off.

My father fired several shots and brought down two birds; Ivan Sergeyevitch had no luck, and was envying my father's good fortune all the time. At last, when it was beginning to get dark, a woodcock flew over Turgenieff, and he shot it.

"Killed it?" called out my father.

"Fell like a stone; send your dog to pick him up," answered Ivan Sergeyevitch.

My father sent us with the dog, Turgenieff showed us where to look for the bird; but search as we might, and the dog, too, there was no woodcock to be found. At last Turgenieff came to help, and my father came; there was no woodcock there.

"Perhaps you only winged it; it may have got away along the ground," said my father, puzzled. "It is impossible that the dog shouldn't find it; he couldn't miss a bird that was killed."

"I tell you I saw it with my own eyes, Lyoff Nikolaievich; it fell like a stone. I didn't wound it; I killed it outright. I can tell the difference."

"Then why can't the dog find it? It's impossible; there's something wrong."

"I don't know anything about that," insisted Turgenieff. "You may take it from me I'm not lying; it fell like a stone where I tell you."

There was no finding the woodcock, and the incident left an unpleasant flavor, as if one or the other of them was in the wrong. Either Turgenieff was bragging when he said that he shot it dead, or my father, in maintaining that the dog could not fail to find a bird that had been killed.

And this must needs happen just when they were both so anxious to avoid every sort of misunderstanding! That was the very reason why they had carefully fought shy of all serious conversation, and spent all their time merely amusing themselves.

When my father said good night to us that night, he whispered to us that we were to get up early and go back to the place to have a good hunt for the bird.

And what was the result? The woodcock, in falling, had caught in the fork of a branch, right at the top of an aspen-tree, and it was all we could do to knock it out from there.

When we brought it home in triumph, it was something of an "occasion," and my father and Turgenieff were far more delighted than we were. It turned out that they were both in the right, and everything ended to their mutual satisfaction.

Ivan Sergeyevitch slept down-stairs in my father's study. When the party broke up for the night, I used to see him to his room, and while he was undressing I sat on his bed and talked sport with him.

He asked me if I could shoot. I said yes, but that I didn't care to go out shooting because I had nothing but a rotten old one-barreled gun.

"I'll give you a gun," he said. "I've got two in Paris, and I have no earthly need for both. It's not an expensive gun, but it's a good one. Next time I come to Russia I'll bring it with me."

I was quite taken aback and thanked him heartily. I was tremendously delighted at the idea that I was to have a real central-fire gun.

Unfortunately, Turgenieff never came to Russia again. I tried afterward to buy the gun he had spoken of from his legatees not in the quality of a central-fire gun, but as Turgenieff's gun; but I did not succeed.

That is all that I can remember about this delightful, naively cordial man, with the childlike eyes and the childlike laugh, and in the picture my mind preserves of him the memory of his grandeur melts into the charm of his good nature and simplicity.

In 1883 my father received from Ivan Sergeyevitch his last farewell letter, written in pencil on his death-bed, and I remember with what emotion he read it. And when the news of his death came, my father would talk of nothing else for several days, and inquired everywhere for details of his illness and last days.

Apropos of this letter of Turgenieff's, I should like to say that my father was sincerely annoyed, when he heard applied to himself the epithet "great writer of the land of Russia," which was taken from this letter.

He always hated cliches, and he regarded this one as quite absurd.

"Why not 'writer of the land'? I never heard before that a man could be the writer of a land. People get attached to some nonsensical expression, and go on repeating it in season and out of season."

I have given extracts above from Turgenieff's letters, which show the invariable consistency with which he lauded my father's literary talents. Unfortunately, I cannot say the same of my father's attitude toward Turgenieff.

In this, too, the want of dispassionateness in his nature revealed itself. Personal relations prevented him from being objective.

In 1867, apropos of Turgenieff's "Smoke," which had just appeared, he wrote to Fet:

There is hardly any love of anything in "Smoke" and hardly any poetry. The only thing it shows love for is light and playful adultery, and for that reason the poetry of the story is repulsive. ... I am timid in expressing this opinion, because I cannot form a sober judgment about an author whose personality I dislike.

In 1865, before the final breach with Turgenieff, he wrote, again to Fet: "I do not like 'Enough'!" A personal subjective treatment is never good unless it is full of life and passion; but the subjectivity in this case is full of lifeless suffering.

In the autumn of 1883, after Turgenieff's death, when the family had gone into Moscow for the winter, my father stayed at Yasnaya Polyana alone, with Agafya Mikhailovna, and set earnestly about reading through all Turgenieff's works.

This is what he wrote to my mother at the time:

I am always thinking about Turgenieff. I am intensely fond of him, and sorry for him, and do nothing but read him. I live entirely with him. I shall certainly give a lecture on him, or write it to be read; tell Yuryef.

"Enough"—read it; it is perfectly charming.

Unfortunately, my father's intended lecture on Turgenieff never came off. The Government forbade him to pay this last tribute to his dead friend, with whom he had quarreled all his life only because he could not be indifferent to him.

(To be continued)

REMINISCENCES OF TOLSTOY (Part III.)

BY HIS SON, COUNT ILYA TOLSTOY

TRANSLATED BY GEORGE CALDERON

AT this point I shall turn back and try to trace the influence which my father had on my upbringing, and I shall recall as well as I can the impressions that he left on my mind in my childhood, and later in the melancholy days of my early manhood, which happened to coincide with the radical change in his whole philosophy of life.

In 1852, tired of life in the Caucasus and remembering his old home at Yasnaya Polyana, he wrote to his aunt, Tatyana Alexandrovna:

After some years, I shall find myself, neither very young nor very old, back at Yasnaya Polyana again: my affairs will all be in order; I shall have no anxieties for the future and no troubles in the present.

You also will be living at Yasnaya. You will be getting a little old, but you will be healthy and vigorous. We shall lead the life we led in the old days; I shall work in the mornings, but we shall meet and see each other almost all day.

We shall dine together in the evening. I shall read you something that interests you. Then we shall talk: I shall tell you about my life in the Caucasus; you will give me reminiscences of my father and mother; you will tell me some of those "terrible stories" to which we used to listen in the old days with frightened eyes and open mouths.

We shall talk about the people that we loved and who are no more.

You will cry, and I, too; but our tears will be refreshing, tranquilizing tears. We shall talk about my brothers, who will visit us from time to time, and about dear Masha, who will also spend several months every year at Yasnaya, which she loves, with all her children.

We shall have no acquaintances; no one will come in to bore us with gossip.

It is a wonderful dream; but that is not all that I let myself dream of.

> I shall be married. My wife will be gentle, kind, and affectionate; she will love you as I do; we shall have children who will call you granny; you will live in the big house, in the same room on the top floor where my grandmother lived before.

The whole house will be run on the same lines as it was in my father's time, and we shall begin the same life over again, but with a change of roles.

You will take my grandmother's place, but you will be better still than she was; I shall take my father's place, though I can never hope to be worthy of the honor.

My wife will take my mother's place, and the children ours.

Masha will fill the part of both my aunts, except for their sorrow; and there will even be Gasha there to take the place of Prashovya Ilyinitchna.

The only thing lacking will be some one to take the part you played in the life of our family. We shall never find such a noble and loving heart as yours. There is no one to succeed you.

There will be three new faces that will appear among us from time to time: my brothers, especially one who will often be with us, Nikolenka, who will be an old bachelor, bald, retired, always the same kindly, noble fellow.

Just ten years after this letter, my father married, and almost all his dreams were realized, just as he had wished. Only the big house, with his grandmother's room, was missing, and his brother Nikolenka, with the dirty hands, for he died two years before, in 1860.

In his family life my father witnessed a repetition of the life of his parents, and in us children he sought to find a repetition of himself and his brothers. We were brought up as regular gentlefolk, proud of our social position and holding aloof from all the outer world. Everything that was not us was below us, and therefore unworthy of imitation. I knew that my father felt very earnestly about the chastity of young people; I knew how much strength he laid on purity. An early marriage seemed to me the best solution of the difficult question that must harass every thoughtful boy when he attains to man's estate.

Two or three years later, when I was eighteen and we were living in Moscow, I fell in love with a young lady I knew, my present wife, and went almost every Saturday to her father's house.

My father knew, but said nothing. One day when he was going out for a walk I asked if I might go with him. As I very seldom went for walks with him in Moscow, he guessed that I wanted to have a serious talk with him about something, and after walking some distance in silence, evidently feeling that I was shy about it and did not like to break the ice, he suddenly began:

"You seem to go pretty often to the F— —s'."

I said that I was very fond of the eldest daughter.

"Oh, do you want to marry her?"

"Yes."

"Is she a good girl? Well, mind you don't make a mistake, and don't be false to her," he said with a curious gentleness and thoughtfulness.

I left him at once and ran back home, delighted, along the Arbat. I was glad that I had told him the truth, and his affectionate and cautious way of taking it strengthened my affection both for him, to whom I was boundlessly grateful for his cordiality, and for her, whom I loved still more warmly from that moment, and to whom I resolved still more fervently never to be untrue.

My father's tactfulness toward us amounted almost to timidity. There were certain questions which he could never bring himself to touch on for fear of causing us pain. I shall never forget how once in

Moscow I found him sitting writing at the table in my room when I dashed in suddenly to change my clothes.

My bed stood behind a screen, which hid him from me.

When he heard my footsteps he said, without looking round:

"Is that you, Ilya?"

"Yes, it's I."

"Are you alone? Shut the door. There's no one to hear us, and we can't see each other, so we shall not feel ashamed. Tell me, did you ever have anything to do with women?"

When I said no, I suddenly heard him break out sobbing, like a little child.

I sobbed and cried, too, and for a long time we stayed weeping tears of joy, with the screen between us, and we were neither of us ashamed, but both so joyful that I look on that moment as one of the happiest in my whole life.

No arguments or homilies could ever have effected what the emotion I experienced at that moment did. Such tears as those shed by a father of sixty can never be forgotten even in moments of the strongest temptation.

My father observed my inward life most attentively between the ages of sixteen and twenty, noted all my doubts and hesitations, encouraged me in my good impulses, and often found fault with me for inconsistency.

I still have some of his letters written at that time. Here are two:

I had just written you, my dear friend Ilya, a letter that was true to my own feelings, but, I am afraid, unjust, and I am not sending it. I said unpleasant things in it, but I have no right to do so. I do not know you as I should like to and as I ought to know you. That is my fault. And I wish to remedy it. I know much in you that I do not like, but I do not know everything. As for your proposed journey home, I think that in your position of student, not only student of a gymnase, but at the age of study, it is better to gad about as little as possible; moreover, all useless expenditure of money that you can easily refrain from is immoral, in my opinion, and in yours, too, if you only consider it. If you come, I shall be glad for my own sake, so long as you are not inseparable from G— —.

Do as you think best. But you must work, both with your head, thinking and reading, and with your heart; that is, find out for yourself what is really good and what is bad, although it seems to be good. I kiss you.

L. T.

Dear Friend Ilya:

There is always somebody or something that prevents me from answering your two letters, which are important and dear to me, especially the last. First it was Baturlin, then bad health, insomnia, then the arrival of D— —, the friend of H— — that I wrote you about. He is sitting at tea talking to the ladies, neither understanding the other; so I left them, and want to write what little I can of all that I think about you.

Even supposing that S— — A— — demands too much of you, 19 there is no harm in waiting; especially from the point of view of fortifying your opinions, your faith. That is the one important thing. If you don't, it is a fearful disaster to put off from one shore and not reach the other.

The one shore is an honest and good life, for your own delight and the profit of others. But there is a bad life, too—a life so sugared, so common to all, that if you follow it, you do not notice that it is a bad life, and suffer only in your conscience, if you have one; but if you leave it, and do not reach the real shore, you will be made miserable by solitude and by the reproach of having deserted your fellows, and you will be ashamed. In short, I want to say that it is out of the question to want to be rather good; it is out of the question to jump into the water unless you know how to swim. One must be truthful and wish to be good with all one's might, too. Do you feel this in you? The drift of what I say is that we all know what PRINCESS MARYA ALEXEVNA 20 verdict about your marriage would be: that if young people marry without a sufficient fortune, it means children, poverty, getting tired of each other in a year or two; in ten years, quarrels, want—hell. And in all this PRINCESS MAR-

YA ALEXEVNA is perfectly right and plays the true prophet, unless these young people who are getting married have another purpose, their one and only one, unknown to PRINCESS MARYA ALEXEVNA, and that not a brainish purpose, not one recognized by the intellect, but one that gives life its color and the attainment of which is more moving than any other. If you have this, good; marry at once, and give the lie to PRINCESS MARYA ALEXEVNA. If not, it is a hundred to one that your marriage will lead to nothing but misery. I am speaking to you from the bottom of my heart. Receive my words into the bottom of yours, and weigh them well. Besides love for you as a son, I have love for you also as a man standing at the cross-ways. I kiss you and Lyolya and Noletchka and Seryozha, if he is back. We are all alive and well.

The following letter belongs to the same period:

Your letter to Tanya has arrived, my dear friend Ilya, and I see that you are still advancing toward that purpose which you set up for yourself; and I want to write to you and to her—for no doubt you tell her everything—what I think about it. Well, I think about it a great deal, with joy and with fear mixed. This is what I think. If one marries in order to enjoy oneself more, no good will ever come of it. To set up as one's main object, ousting everything else, marriage, union with the being you love, is a great mistake. And an obvious one, if you think about it. Object, marriage. Well, you marry; and what then? If you had no other object in life before your marriage, it will be twice as hard to find one.

As a rule, people who are getting married completely forget this.

So many joyful events await them in the future, in wedlock and the arrival of children, that those events seem to constitute life itself. But this is indeed a dangerous illusion.

If parents merely live from day to day, begetting children, and have no purpose in life, they are only putting off the question of the purpose of life and that punishment which is allotted to people who live without knowing why; they are only putting it off and not escaping it, because they will have to bring up their children and guide their steps, but they will have nothing to guide them by. And then the parents lose their human qualities and the happiness which depends on the possession of them, and turn into mere breeding cattle.

That is why I say that people who are proposing to marry because their life SEEMS to them to be full must more than ever set themselves to think and make clear to their own minds for the sake of what each of them lives.

And in order to make this clear, you must consider the circumstances in which you live, your past. Reckon up what you consider important and what unimportant in life. Find out what you believe in; that is, what you look on as eternal and immutable truth, and what you will take for your guide in life. And not only find out, but make clear to your own mind, and try to practise or to learn to practise in your daily life; because until you practise what you believe you cannot tell whether you believe it or not.

I know your faith, and that faith, or those sides of it which can be expressed in deeds, you must now more than ever make clear to your own mind, by putting them into practice.

Your faith is that your welfare consists in loving people and being loved by them. For the attainment of this end I know of three lines of action in which I perpetually exercise myself, in which one can never exercise oneself enough and which are specially necessary to you now.

First, in order to be able to love people and to be loved by them, one must accustom oneself to expect as little as possible from them, and that is very hard work; for if I expect much, and am often disappointed, I am inclined rather to reproach them than to love them.

Second, in order to love people not in words, but in deed, one must train oneself to do what benefits them. That needs still harder work, especially at your age, when it is one's natural business to be studying.

Third, in order to love people and to b. l. b. t., 21 one must train oneself to gentleness, humility, the art of bearing with disagreeable people and things, the art of behaving to them so as not to offend any one, of being able to choose the least offense. And this is the hardest work of all—work that never ceases from the time you wake till the time you go to sleep, and the most joyful work of all, because day after day you rejoice in your growing success in it, and receive a further reward, unperceived at first, but very joyful after, in being loved by others.

So I advise you, Friend Ilya, and both of you, to live and to think as sincerely as you can, because it is the only way you can discover if you are really going along the same road, and whether it is wise to join hands or not; and at the same time, if you are sincere, you must be making your future ready.

Your purpose in life must not be the joy of wedlock, but, by your life to bring more love and truth into the world. The object of marriage is to help one another in the attainment of that purpose.

The vilest and most selfish life is the life of the people who have joined together only in order to enjoy life; and the highest vocation in the world is that of those who live in order to serve God by bringing good into the world, and who have joined together for that very purpose. Don't mistake half-measures for the real thing. Why should a man not choose the highest? Only when you have chosen the highest, you must set your whole heart on it, and not just a little. Just a little leads to nothing. There, I am tired of writing, and still have much left that I wanted to say. I kiss you.

HELP FOR THE FAMINE-STRICKEN

AFTER my father had come to the conclusion that it was not only useless to help people with money, but immoral, the part he took in distributing food among the peasants during the famines of 1890, 1891, and 1898 may seem to have shown inconsistency and contradiction of thought.

"If a horseman sees that his horse is tired out, he must not remain seated on its back and hold up its head, but simply get off," he used to say, condemning all the charities of the well-fed people who sit on the back of the working classes, continue to enjoy all the benefits of their privileged position, and merely give from their superfluity.

He did not believe in the good of such charity and considered it a form of self-hallucination, all the more harmful because people thereby acquire a sort of moral right to continue that idle, aristocratic life and get to go on increasing the poverty of the people.

In the autumn of 1890 my father thought of writing an article on the famine, which had then spread over nearly all Russia.

Although from the newspapers and from the accounts brought by those who came from the famine-stricken parts he already knew about the extent of the peasantry's disaster, nevertheless, when his old friend Ivanovitch Rayovsky called on him at Yasnaya Polyana and proposed that he should drive through to the Dankovski District with him in order to see the state of things in the villages for himself, he readily agreed, and went with him to his property at Begitchovka.

He went there with the intention of staying only for a day or two; but when he saw what a call there was for immediate measures, he at once set to work to help Rayovsky, who had already instituted several kitchens in the villages, in relieving the distress of the peasantry, at first on a small scale, and then, when big subscriptions began to pour in from every side, on a continually increasing one. The upshot of it was that he devoted two whole years of his life to the work.

It is wrong to think that my father showed any inconsistency in this matter. He did not delude himself for a moment into thinking he was engaged on a virtuous and momentous task, but when he saw the sufferings of the people, he simply could not bear to go on living comfortably at Yasnaya or in Moscow any longer, but had to go out and help in order to relieve his own feelings. Once he wrote:

There is much about it that is not what it ought to be; there is S. A.'s money 22 and the subscriptions; there is the relation of those who feed and those who are fed. THERE IS SIN WITHOUT END, but I cannot stay at home and write. I feel the necessity of taking part in it, of doing something.

Six years later I worked again at the same job with my father in Tchornski and Mtsenski districts.

After the bad crops of the two preceding years it became clear by the beginning of the winter of 1898 that a new famine was approaching in our neighborhood, and that charitable assistance to the peasantry would be needed. I turned to my father for help. By the spring he had managed to collect some money, and at the beginning of April he came himself to see me.

I must say that my father, who was very economical by nature, was extraordinarily cautious and, I may say, even parsimonious in charitable matters. It is of course easy to understand, if one considers the unlimited confidence which he enjoyed among the subscribers and the great moral responsibility which he could not but feel toward them. So that before undertaking anything he had himself to be fully convinced of the necessity of giving aid.

The day after his arrival, we saddled a couple of horses and rode out. We rode as we had ridden together twenty years before, when we went out coursing with our greyhounds; that is, across country, over the fields.

It was all the same to me which way we rode, as I believed that all the neighboring villages were equally distressed, and my father, for the sake of old memories, wanted to revisit Spasskoye Lyutovinovo, which was only six miles from me, and where he had not been since Turgenieff's death. On the way there I remember he told me all about Turgenieff's mother, who was famous through all the neighborhood for her remarkable intelligence, energy, and craziness. I do not know that he ever saw her himself, or whether he was telling me only the reports that he had heard.

As we rode across the Turgenieff's park, he recalled in passing how of old he and Ivan Sergeyevitch had disputed which park was best, Spasskoye or Yasnaya Polyana. I asked him:

"And now which do you think?"

"Yasnaya Polyana IS the best, though this is very fine, very fine indeed."

In the village we visited the head-man's and two or three other cottages, and came away disappointed. There was no famine.

The peasants, who had been endowed at the emancipation with a full share of good land, and had enriched themselves since by wage-earnings, were hardly in want at all. It is true that some of the yards were badly stocked; but there was none of that acute degree of want which amounts to famine and which strikes the eye at once.

I even remember my father reproaching me a little for having sounded the alarm when there was no sufficient cause for it, and for a little while I felt rather ashamed and awkward before him.

Of course when he talked to the peasants he asked each of them if he remembered Turgenieff and eagerly picked up anything they had to say about him. Some of the old men remembered him and spoke of him with great affection.

MY FATHER'S ILLNESS IN THE CRIMEA

IN the autumn of 1901 my father was attacked by persistent feverishness, and the doctors advised him to spend the winter in the Crimea. Countess Panina kindly lent him her Villa Gaspra, near Koreiz, and he spent the winter there.

Soon after his arrival, he caught cold and had two illnesses one after the other, enteric fever and inflammation of the lungs. At one time his condition was so bad that the doctors had hardly any hope that he would ever rise from his bed again. Despite the fact that his temperature went up very high, he was conscious all the time; he dictated some reflections every day, and deliberately prepared for death.

The whole family was with him, and we all took turns in helping to nurse him. I look back with pleasure on the nights when it fell to me to be on duty by him, and I sat in the balcony by the open window, listening to his breathing and every sound in his room. My chief duty, as the strongest of the family, was to lift him up while the sheets were being changed. When they were making the bed, I had to hold him in my arms like a child.

I remember how my muscles quivered one day with the exertion. He looked at me with astonishment and said:

"You surely don't find me heavy? What nonsense!"

I thought of the day when he had given me a bad time at riding in the woods as a boy, and kept asking, "You're not tired?"

Another time during the same illness he wanted me to carry him down-stairs in my arms by the winding stone staircase.

"Pick me up as they do a baby and carry me."

He had not a grain of fear that I might stumble and kill him. It was all I could do to insist on his being carried down in an arm-chair by three of us.

Was my father afraid of death?

It is impossible to answer the question in one word. With his tough constitution and physical strength, he always instinctively fought not only against death, but against old age. Till the last year of his life he never gave in, but always did everything for himself and even rode on horseback.

To suppose, therefore, that he had no instinctive fear of death is out of the question. He had that fear, and in a very high degree, but he was constantly fighting to overcome it.

Did he succeed?

I can answer definitely yes. During his illness he talked a great deal of death and prepared himself for it firmly and deliberately. When he felt that he was getting weaker, he wished to say good-by to everybody, and he called us all separately to his bedside, one after the other, and gave his last words of advice to each. He was so weak that he spoke in a half-whisper, and when he had said good-by to one, he had to rest for a while and collect his strength for the rest.

When my turn came, he said as nearly as I can remember:

"You are still young and strong and tossed by storms of passion. You have not therefore yet been able to think over the chief questions of life. But this stage will pass. I am sure of it. When the time comes, believe me, you will find the truth in the teachings of the

Gospel. I am dying peacefully simply because I have come to know that teaching and believe in it. May God grant you this knowledge soon! Good-by."

I kissed his hand and left the room quietly. When I got to the front door, I rushed to a lonely stone tower, and there sobbed my heart out in the darkness like a child. Looking round at last, I saw that some one else was sitting on the staircase near me, also crying.

So I said farewell to my father years before his death, and the memory of it is dear to me, for I know that if I had seen him before his death at Astapova he would have said just the same to me.

To return to the question of death, I will say that so far from being afraid of it, in his last days he often desired it; he was more interested in it than afraid of it. This "greatest of mysteries" interested him to such a degree that his interest came near to love. How eagerly he listened to accounts of the death of his friends, Turgenieff, Gay, Leskof, 23 Zhemtchuzhnikof 24; and others! He inquired after the smallest matters; no detail, however trifling in appearance, was without its interest and importance to him.

His "Circle of Reading," November 7, the day he died, is devoted entirely to thoughts on death.

"Life is a dream, death is an awakening," he wrote, while in expectation of that awakening.

Apropos of the "Circle of Reading," I cannot refrain from relating a characteristic incident which I was told by one of my sisters.

When my father had made up his mind to compile that collection of the sayings of the wise, to which he gave the name of "Circle of Reading," he told one of his friends about it.

A few days afterward this friend came to see him again, and at once told him that he and his wife had been thinking over his scheme for the new book and had come to the conclusion that he ought to call it "For Every Day," instead of "Circle of Reading."

To this my father replied that he preferred the title "Circle of Reading" because the word "circle" suggested the idea of continuous reading, which was what he meant to express by the title.

Half an hour later the friend came across the room to him and repeated exactly the same remark again. This time my father made no reply. In the evening, when the friend was preparing to go home, as he was saying good-by to my father, he held his hand in his and began once more:

"Still, I must tell you, Lyoff Nikolaievich, that I and my wife have been thinking it over, and we have come to the conclusion," and so on, word for word the same.

"No, no, I want to die—to die as soon as possible," groaned my father when he had seen the friend off.

"Isn't it all the same whether it's 'Circle of Reading' or 'For Every Day'? No, it's time for me to die: I cannot live like this any longer."

And, after all, in the end, one of the editions of the sayings of the wise was called "For Every Day" instead of "Circle of Reading."

"Ah, my dear, ever since this Mr. —— turned up, I really don't know which of Lyoff Nikolaievich's writings are by Lyoff Nikolaievich and which are by Mr. ——!" murmured our old friend, the pure-hearted and far from malicious Marya Alexandrovna Schmidt.

This sort of intrusion into my father's work as an author bore, in the "friend's" language, the modest title of "corrections beforehand," and there is no doubt that Marya Alexandrovna was right, for no one will ever know where what my father wrote ends and where his concessions to Mr. ——'s persistent "corrections beforehand" begin, all the more as this careful adviser had the forethought to arrange that when my father answered his letters he was always to return him the letters they were answers to.25

Besides the desire for death that my father displayed, in the last years of his life he cherished another dream, which he made no secret of his hope of realizing, and that was the desire to suffer for his convictions. The first impulse in this direction was given him by the persecution on the part of the authorities to which, during his lifetime, many of his friends and fellow-thinkers were subjected.

When he heard of any one being put in jail or deported for disseminating his writings, he was so disturbed about it that one was really sorry for him. I remember my arrival at Yasnaya some days after Gusef's arrest.26 I stayed two days with my father, and heard of nothing but Gusef. As if there were nobody in the world but Gusef! I must confess that, sorry as I was for Gusef, who was shut up at the time in the local prison at Krapivna, I harbored a most wicked feeling of resentment at my father's paying so little attention to me and the rest of those about him and being so absorbed in the thought of Gusef.

I willingly acknowledge that I was wrong in entertaining this narrow-minded feeling. If I had entered fully into what my father was feeling, I should have seen this at the time.

As far back as 1896, in consequence of the arrest of a doctor, Miss N— —, in Tula, my father wrote a long letter to Muravyof, the Minister of Justice, in which he spoke of the "unreasonableness, uselessness, and cruelty of the measures taken by the Government against those who disseminate these forbidden writings," and begged him to "direct the measures taken to punish or intimidate the perpetrators of the evil, or to put an end to it, against the man whom you regard as the real instigator of it... all the more, as I assure you beforehand, that I shall continue without ceasing till my death to do what the Government considers evil and what I consider my sacred duty before God."

As every one knows, neither this challenge nor the others that followed it led to any result, and the arrests and deportations of those associated with him still went on.

My father felt himself morally responsible toward all those who suffered on his account, and every year new burdens were laid on his conscience.

MASHA'S DEATH

As I reach the description of the last days of my father's life, I must once more make it clear that what I write is based only on the personal impressions I received in my periodical visits to Yasnaya Polyana.

Unfortunately, I have no rich shorthand material to rely on, such as Gusef and Bulgakof had for their memoirs, and more especially Dushan Petrovitch Makowicki, who is preparing, I am told, a big and conscientious work, full of truth and interest.

In November, 1906, my sister Masha died of inflammation of the lungs. It is a curious thing that she vanished out of life with just as little commotion as she had passed through it. Evidently this is the lot of all the pure in heart.

No one was particularly astonished by her death. I remember that when I received the telegram, I felt no surprise. It seemed perfectly natural to me. Masha had married a kinsman of ours, Prince Obolenski; she lived on her own estate at Pirogovo, twenty-one miles from us, and spent half the year with her husband at Yasnaya. She was very delicate and had constant illnesses.

When I arrived at Yasnaya the day after her death, I was aware of an atmosphere of exaltation and prayerful emotion about the whole family, and it was then I think for the first time that I realized the full grandeur and beauty of death.

I definitely felt that by her death Masha, so far from having gone away from us, had come nearer to us, and had been, as it were, welded to us forever in a way that she never could have been during her lifetime.

I observed the same frame of mind in my father. He went about silent and woebegone, summoning all his strength to battle with his own sorrow; but I never heard him utter a murmur of a complaint, only words of tender emotion. When the coffin was carried to the church he changed his clothes and went with the cortege. When he reached the stone pillars he stopped us, said farewell to the departed, and walked home along the avenue. I looked after him and watched him walk away across the wet, thawing snow with his short, quick old man's steps, turning his toes out at a sharp angle, as he always did, and never once looking round.

My sister Masha had held a position of great importance in my father's life and in the life of the whole family. Many a time in the last few years have we had occasion to think of her and to murmur sadly: "If only Masha had been with us! If only Masha had not died!"

In order to explain the relations between Masha and my father I must turn back a considerable way. There was one distinguishing and, at first sight, peculiar trait in my father's character, due perhaps to the fact that he grew up without a mother, and that was that all exhibitions of tenderness were entirely foreign to him.

I say "tenderness" in contradistinction to heartiness. Heartiness he had and in a very high degree.

His description of the death of my Uncle Nikolai is characteristic in this connection. In a letter to his other brother, Sergei Nikolayevitch, in which he described the last day of his brother's life, my father tells how he helped him to undress.

"He submitted, and became a different man.... He had a word of praise for everybody, and said to me, 'Thanks, my friend.' You understand the significance of the words as between us two."

It is evident that in the language of the Tolstoy brothers the phrase "my friend" was an expression of tenderness beyond which imagination could not go. The words astonished my father even on the lips of his dying brother.

During all his lifetime I never received any mark of tenderness from him whatever.

He was not fond of kissing children, and when he did so in saying good morning or good night, he did it merely as a duty.

It is therefore easy to understand that he did not provoke any display of tenderness toward himself, and that nearness and dearness with him were never accompanied by any outward manifestations.

It would never have come into my head, for instance, to walk up to my father and kiss him or to stroke his hand. I was partly prevented also from that by the fact that I always looked up to him with awe, and his spiritual power, his greatness, prevented me from seeing in him the mere man—the man who was so plaintive and weary at times, the feeble old man who so much needed warmth and rest.

The only person who could give him that warmth was Masha.

She would go up to him, stroke his hand, caress him, and say something affectionate, and you could see that he liked it, was happy, and even responded in kind. It was as if he became a different man with her. Why was it that Masha was able to do this, while no one else even dared to try? If any other of us had done it, it would have seemed unnatural, but Masha could do it with perfect simplicity and sincerity.

I do not mean to say that others about my father loved him less than Masha; not at all; but the display of love for him was never so warm and at the same time so natural with any one else as with her.

So that with Masha's death my father was deprived of this natural source of warmth, which, with advancing years, had become more and more of a necessity for him.

Another and still greater power that she possessed was her remarkably delicate and sensitive conscience. This trait in her was still dearer to my father than her caresses.

How good she was at smoothing away all misunderstandings! How she always stood up for those who were found any fault with, justly or unjustly! It was all the same to her. Masha could reconcile everybody and everything.

During the last years of his life my father's health perceptibly grew worse. Several times he had the most sudden and inexplicable sort of fainting fits, from which he used to recover the next day, but completely lost his memory for a time.

Seeing my brother Andrei's children, who were staying at Yasnaya, in the zala one day, he asked with some surprise, "Whose children are these?" Meeting my wife, he said, "Don't be offended, my dear; I know that I am very fond of you, but I have quite forgotten who you are"; and when he went up to the zala after one of these fainting fits, he looked round with an astonished air and said, "Where's my brother Nitenka." Nitenka had died fifty years before.

The day following all traces of the attack would disappear.

During one of these fainting fits my brother Sergei, in undressing my father, found a little note-book on him. He put it in his own pocket, and next day, when he came to see my father, he handed it back to him, telling him that he had not read it.

"There would have been no harm in YOUR seeing it," said my father, as he took it back.

This little diary in which he wrote down his most secret thoughts and prayers was kept "for himself alone," and he never showed it to any one. I saw it after my father's death. It is impossible to read it without tears.

It is curious that the sudden decay of my father's memory displayed itself only in the matter of real facts and people. He was entirely unaffected in his literary work, and everything that he wrote down to the last days of his life is marked by his characteristic logicalness and force. It may be that the reason he forgot the details of real life was because he was too deeply absorbed in his abstract work.

My wife was at Yasnaya Polyana in October, and when she came home she told me that there was something wrong there. "Your mother is nervous and hysterical; your father is in a silent and gloomy frame of mind."

I was very busy with my office work, but made up my mind to devote my first free day to going and seeing my father and mother.

When I got to Yasnaya, my father had already left it.

I paid Aunt Masha a visit some little time after my father's funeral. We sat together in her comfortable little cell, and she repeated to me once more in detail the oft-repeated story of my father's last visit to her.

"He sat in that very arm-chair where you are sitting now, and how he cried!" she said.

"When Sasha arrived with her girl friend, they set to work studying this map of Russia and planning out a route to the Caucasus. Lyovotchka sat there thoughtful and melancholy.

"'Never mind, Papa; it'll be all right,' said Sasha, trying to encourage him.

"'Ah, you women, you women!' answered her father, bitterly. 'How can it ever be all right?'

"I so much hoped that he would settle down here; it would just have suited him. And it was his own idea, too; he had even taken a cottage in the village," Aunt Masha sadly recalled.

"When he left me to go back to the hotel where he was staying, it seemed to me that he was rather calmer.

"When he said good-by, he even made some joke about his having come to the wrong door.

"I certainly would never have imagined that he would go away again that same night."

It was a grievous trial for Aunt Masha when the old confessor Iosif, who was her spiritual director, forbade her to pray for her dead brother because he had been excommunicated. She was too broad-minded to be able to reconcile herself to the harsh intolerance of the church, and for a time she was honestly indignant. Another priest to whom she applied also refused her request.

Marya Nikolayevna could not bring herself to disobey her spiritual fathers, but at the same time she felt that she was not really obeying their injunction, for she prayed for him all the same, in thought, if not in words.

There is no knowing how her internal discord would have ended if her father confessor, evidently understanding the moral torment she was suffering, had not given her permission to pray for her brother, but only in her cell and in solitude, so as not to lead others astray.

MY FATHER'S WILL. CONCLUSION

ALTHOUGH my father had long since renounced the copyright in all his works written after 1883, and although, after having made all his real estate over to his children, he had, as a matter of fact, no property left, still he could not but be aware that his life was far from corresponding to his principles, and this consciousness perpetually preyed upon his mind. One has only to read some of his posthumous works attentively to see that the idea of leaving home and radically altering his whole way of life had presented itself to him long since and was a continual temptation to him.

This was the cherished dream that always allured him, but which he did not think himself justified in putting into practice.

The life of the Christian must be a "reasonable and happy life IN ALL POSSIBLE CIRCUMSTANCES," he used to say as he struggled with the temptation to go away, and gave up his own soul for others.

I remember reading in Gusef's memoirs how my father once, in conversation with Gusoryof, the peasant, who had made up his mind to leave his home for religious reasons, said, "My life is a hundred thousand times more loathsome than yours, but yet I cannot leave it."

I shall not enumerate all the letters of abuse and amazement which my father received from all sides, upbraiding him with luxury, with inconsistency, and even with torturing his peasants. It is easy to imagine what an impression they made on him.

He said there was good reason to revile him; he called their abuse "a bath for the soul," but internally he suffered from the "bath," and saw no way out of his difficulties. He bore his cross, and it was in this self-renunciation that his power consisted, though many either could not or would not understand it. He alone, despite all those about him, knew that this cross was laid on him not of man, but of God; and while he was strong, he loved his burden and shared it with none.

Just as thirty years before he had been haunted by the temptation to suicide, so now he struggled with a new and more powerful temptation, that of flight.

A few days before he left Yasnaya he called on Marya Alexandrovna Schmidt at Ovsyanniki and confessed to her that he wanted to go away.

The old lady held up her hands in horror and said:

"Gracious Heavens, Lyoff Nikolaievich, have you come to such a pitch of weakness?"

When I learned, on October 28, 1910, that my father had left Yasnaya, the same idea occurred to me, and I even put it into words in a letter I sent to him at Shamerdino by my sister Sasha.

I did not know at the time about certain circumstances which have since made a great deal clear to me that was obscure before.

From the moment of my father's death till now I have been racking my brains to discover what could have given him the impulse to take that last step. What power could compel him to yield in the struggle in which he had held firmly and tenaciously for many years? What was the last drop, the last grain of sand that turned the scales, and sent him forth to search for a new life on the very edge of the grave?

Could he really have fled from home because the wife that he had lived with for forty-eight years had developed neurasthenia and at one time showed certain abnormalities characteristic of that malady? Was that like the man who so loved his fellows and so well knew the human heart? Or did he suddenly desire, when he was eighty-three, and weak and helpless, to realize the idea of a pilgrim's life?

If so, why did he take my sister Sasha and Dr. Makowicki with him? He could not but know that in their company he would be just as well provided with all the necessaries of life as he would have been at Yasnaya Polyana. It would have been the most palpable self-deception.

Knowing my father as I did, I felt that the question of his flight was not so simple as it seemed to others, and the problem lay long unsolved before me until it was suddenly made clear by the will that he left behind him.

I remember how, after N. S. Leskof's death, my father read me his posthumous instructions with regard to a pauper funeral, with no speeches at the grave, and so on, and how the idea of writing his own will then came into his head for the first time.

His first will was written in his diary, on March 27, 1895. 27

The fourth paragraph, to which I wish to call particular attention, contains a request to his next of kin to transfer the right of publishing his writings to society at large, or, in other words, to renounce the copyright of them.

"But I only request it, and do not direct it. It is a good thing to do. And it will be good for you to do it; but if you do not do it, that is your affair. It means that you are not yet ready to do it. The fact that my writings have been bought and sold during these last ten years has been the most painful thing in my whole life to me."

Three copies were made of this will, and they were kept by my sister Masha, my brother Sergei, and Tchertkof.

I knew of its existence, but I never saw it till after my father's death, and I never inquired of anybody about the details.

I knew my father's views about copyright, and no will of his could have added anything to what I knew. I knew, moreover, that this will was not properly executed according to the forms of law, and personally I was glad of that, for I saw in it another proof of my father's confidence in his family. I need hardly add that I never doubted that my father's wishes would be carried out.

My sister Masha, with whom I once had a conversation on the subject, was of the same opinion.

In 1909 my father stayed with Mr. Tchertkof at Krekshin, and there for the first time he wrote a formal will, attested by the signature of witnesses. How this will came to be written I do not know, and I do not intend to discuss it. It afterward appeared that it also was imperfect from a legal point of view, and in October, 1909, it had all to be done again.

As to the writing of the third we are fully informed by Mr. F. Strakhof in an article which he published in the St. Petersburg "Gazette" on November 6, 1911.

Mr. Strakhof left Moscow at night. He had calculated on Sofya Andreyevna, 28 whose presence at Yasnaya Polyana was highly inexpedient for the business on which he was bound, being still in Moscow.

The business in question, as was made clear in the preliminary consultation which V. G. Tchertkof held with N. K. Muravyof, the solicitor, consisted in getting fresh signatures from Lyoff Nikolaievich, whose great age made it desirable to make sure, without delay, of his wishes being carried out by means of a more unassailable legal document. Strakhof brought the draft of the will with him, and laid it before Lyoff Nikolaievich. After reading the paper through, he at once wrote under it that he agreed with its purport, and then added, after a pause:

"All this business is very disagreeable to me, and it is unnecessary. To insure the propagation of my ideas by taking all sorts of measures—why, no word can perish without leaving its trace, if it expresses a truth, and if the man who utters it believes profoundly in its truth. But all these outward means for insuring it only come of our disbelief in what we utter."

And with these words Lyoff Nikolaievich left the study.

Thereupon Mr. Strakhof began to consider what he must do next, whether he should go back with empty hands, or whether he should argue it out.

He decided to argue it out, and endeavored to explain to my father how painful it would be for his friends after his death to hear people blaming him for not having taken any steps, despite his strong opinion on the subject, to see that his wishes were carried out, and for having thereby helped to transfer his copyrights to the members of his family.

Tolstoy promised to think it over, and left the room again.

At dinner Sofya Andreyevna "was evidently far from having any suspicions." When Tolstoy was not by, however, she asked Mr. Strakhof what he had come down about. Inasmuch as Mr. Strakhof had other affairs in hand besides the will, he told her about one thing and another with an easy conscience.

Mr. Strakhof described a second visit to Yasnaya, when he came to attest the same will as a witness.

When he arrived, he said: "The countess had not yet come down. I breathed again."

Of his departure, he said:

As I said good-by to Sofya Andreyevna, I examined her countenance attentively. Such complete tranquillity and cordiality toward her departing guests were written on it that I had not the smallest doubt of her complete ignorance of what was going on.... I left the house with the pleasing consciousness of a work well done—a work that was destined to have a considerable historic consequence. I only felt some little twinge within, certain qualms of conscience about the conspiratorial character of the transaction.

But even this text of the will did not quite satisfy my father's "friends and advisers"; it was redrafted for the fourth and last time in July, 1910.

This last draft was written by my father himself in the Limonovski Forest, two miles from the house, not far from Mr. Tchertkof's estate.

Such is the melancholy history of this document, which was destined to have historic consequences. "All this business is very disagreeable to me, and it is unnecessary," my father said when he signed the paper that was thrust before him. That was his real opinion about his will, and it never altered to the end of his days.

Is there any need of proof for that? I think one need know very little of his convictions to have no doubt about it.

Was Lyoff Nikolaievich Tolstoy likely of his own accord to have recourse to the protection of the law? And, if he did, was he likely to conceal it from his wife and children?

He had been put into a position from which there was absolutely no way out. To tell his wife was out of the question; it would have grievously offended his friends. To have destroyed the will would have been worse still; for his friends had suffered for his principles morally, and some of them materially, and had been exiled from Russia. He felt himself bound to them.

And on the top of all this were his fainting fits, his increasing loss of memory, the clear consciousness of the approach of death, and the continually growing nervousness of his wife, who felt in her heart of hearts the unnatural estrangement of her husband, and could not understand it. If she asked him what it was that he was concealing from her, he would either have to say nothing or to tell her the truth. But that was impossible.

So it came about that the long-cherished dream of leaving Yasnaya Polyana presented itself as the only means of escape. It was certainly not in order to enjoy the full realization of his dream that he left his home; he went away only as a choice of evils.

"I am too feeble and too old to begin a new life," he had said to my brother Sergei only a few days before his departure.

Harassed, ill in body and in mind, he started forth without any object in view, without any thought-out plan, merely in order to hide himself somewhere, wherever it might be, and get some rest from the moral tortures which had become insupportable to him.

"To fly, to fly!" he said in his deathbed delirium as he lay at Astapova.

"Has papa considered that mama may not survive the separation from him?" I asked my sister Sasha on October 29, when she was on the point of going to join him at Shamerdino.

"Yes, he has considered all that, and still made up his mind to go, because he thinks that nothing could be worse than the state that things have come to here," she answered.

I confess that my explanation of my father's flight by no means exhausts the question. Life is complex and every explanation of a man's conduct is bound to suffer from one-sidedness. Besides, there are circumstances of which I do not care to speak at the present moment, in order not to cause unnecessary pain to people still living. It may be that if those who were about my father during the last years of his life had known what they were doing, things would have turned out differently.

The years will pass. The accumulated incrustations which hide the truth will pass away. Much will be wiped out and forgotten. Among other things my father's will will be forgotten—that will which he himself looked upon as an "unnecessary outward means." And men will see more clearly that legacy of love and truth in which he believed deeply, and which, according to his own words, "cannot perish without a trace."

In conclusion I cannot refrain from quoting the opinion of one of my kinsmen, who, after my father's death, read the diaries kept both by my father and my mother during the autumn before Lyoff Nikolaievich left Yasnaya Polyana.

"What a terrible misunderstanding!" he said. "Each loved the other with such poignant affection, each was suffering all the time on the other's behalf, and then this terrible ending!... I see the hand of fate in this."